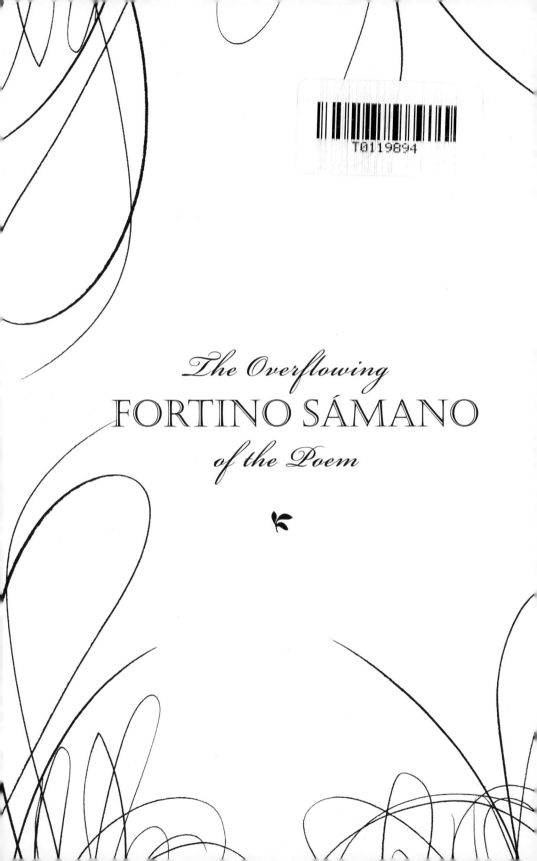

The Overflowing
FORTINO SÁMANO
of the Poem

Virginie Lalucq   Jean-Luc Nancy

FORTINO SÁMANO

(The Overflowing of the Poem)

TRANSLATED BY
SYLVAIN GALLAIS AND CYNTHIA HOGUE

OMNIDAWN PUBLISHING
RICHMOND, CALIFORNIA
2012

Cover Art: LIVE TRANSMISSION: movement of the hands of pianist Martha Argerich
while performing Beethoven's Piano Concerto No. 1. 2002.
Graphite on Bristol paper. 28 x 40 inches. www.MorganOHara.com.
© Copyright Morgan O'Hara.

Book cover and interior design by Cassandra Smith

green press
INITIATIVE

Omnidawn Publishing is committed to preserving ancient
forests and natural resources. We elected to print this title on
30% postconsumer recycled paper, processed chlorine-free. As
a result, for this printing, we have saved:

5 Trees (40' tall and 6-8" diameter)
2,153 Gallons of Wastewater
2 million BTUs of Total Energy
137 Pounds of Solid Waste
477 Pounds of Greenhouse Gases

Omnidawn Publishing made this paper choice because our
printer, Thomson-Shore, Inc., is a member of Green Press
Initiative, a nonprofit program dedicated to supporting authors,
publishers, and suppliers in their efforts to reduce their use of
fiber obtained from endangered forests.

For more information, visit www.greenpressinitiative.org

Environmental impact estimates were made using the Environmental Defense
Paper Calculator. For more information visit: www.edf.org/papercalculator

Library of Congress Cataloging-in-Publication Data

Lalucq, Virginie.
 [Fortino Sámano. English]
 Fortino Sámano : the overflowing of the poem / Virginie Lalucq, Jean-Luc Nancy ;
  translated by Sylvain Gallais and Cynthia Hogue.
   p. cm.
 ISBN 978-1-890650-67-4 (pbk. : alk. paper)
 I. Nancy, Jean-Luc. II. Gallais, Sylvain. III. Hogue, Cynthia. IV. Title.
 PQ2712.A47F6713 2012
 841'.92--dc23

                2012014450

Published by Omnidawn Publishing, Richmond, California
www.omnidawn.com   (510) 237-5472   (800) 792-4957
10 9 8 7 6 5 4 3 2 1
ISBN: 978-1-890650-67-4

ACKNOWLEDGMENTS

Thanks to the editors of Omnidawn for their belief in and enthusiasm about this project, and to the editors of the following journals for publishing selected translations from the poems of Virginie Lalucq together with the translations of the poetic commentaries by Jean-Luc Nancy, sometimes in earlier versions, and sometimes in special guest edited sections:

American Letters and Commentary: "from *Fortino Sámano*" (four poems)
Aufgabe: "from *Fortino Sámano*" (five poems)
Interim: "from *Fortino Sámano*" (four poems)
Lo-Ball: "from *Fortino Sámano*" (four poems)
Parthenon West Review: "from *Fortino Sámano*" (four poems)
Poetry International: "from *Fortino Sámano*" (four poems)
Slope: "from *Fortino Sámano*" (five poems)

A funded faculty leave from the Department of English at Arizona State University (ASU) and a Residency Fellowship from the MacDowell Colony helped Cynthia Hogue to advance these translations. A sabbatical leave from ASU and a Witter Bynner Translation Residency Fellowship from the Santa Fe Art Institute helped her to complete them. In addition, Faculty Development grants from the Virginia G. Piper Center for Creative Writing and the Maxine and Jonathan Marshall Endowment helped fund on-site research and in-person consultations with Virginie Lalucq crucial to progress on this book-length translation. The translators are grateful to all of these organizations, as well as to their directors and staffs, for the precious gifts of time and money.

The translators also wish to extend their thanks to the following individuals who helped them at various stages: Julia Zarankin, Marie-Ange and Daniel Gigot, Cole Swensen, Sarah Riggs, Martha Collins, Aliki Barnstone, Christopher Burawa, Alberto Rios, Joanna Delorme and Cécile Bourguignon of Éditions Galilée, Chad Sweeney, Paul Morris, and to Hogue's 2010 graduate class in Literary Translation, all thanks for your engaged work and brainstorming about translation: you were an inspiration!

Finally, to Virginie Lalucq, with whom we consulted closely on occasion over the years, and Jean-Luc Nancy, who gave us the green light on this project all along, we are grateful to you for trusting us with your works. We hope to have conveyed something of their essence in transporting them into English.

Grateful acknowledgment is given to the following sources for permission to reprint:

Fortino Sámano (*Les débordements du poème*) by Virginie Lalucq and Jean-Luc Nancy. Copyright © 2004 by Éditions Galilée. Used by permission of the authors and Éditions Galilée.

"Aphasia," from *some thing black*, by Jacques Roubaud. Trans. from the French by Rosmarie Waldrop from Dalkey Archive Press (1990). Originally published by Éditions Gallimard as *Quelque chose noir*, 1986, copyright © 1986 by Éditions Gallimard. English translation copyright © 1990 Rosmarie Waldrop. Reprinted with permission of Dalkey Archive Press and Rosmarie Waldrop.

FOREWORD
13

FORTINO SÁMANO
by Virginie Lalucq
A series of thirty-nine untitled poems
(the French original facing the English translation)
16

THE OVERFLOWING OF THE POEM
by Jean-Luc Nancy
A series of forty-two untitled commentaries
(the French original facing the English translation)
100

AFTERWORD
191

Translators' Foreword

On a July evening some time ago, we two translators waited in a Paris café for the avant-garde poet (and new mother) Virginie Lalucq, whose book-length poem, *Fortino Sámano*, we had been translating for several years. We'd been early. Soon it would be *l'heure bleue*. Lalucq was quite late, so we ordered another tea, checked our list of questions again. We wondered when, if she'd been held up, we would be getting to Paris again to consult her.

Lalucq is part of a generation of experimental women poets in France who often work collaboratively, and who draw their material from a wide range of sources and languages, working in the tradition of collage and assemblage but with a nuanced and gendered sensibility. A philosopher in particular of aesthetics, Jean-Luc Nancy is Distinguished Professor of Philosophy at the Université Marc Bloch, Strasbourg. Author of many books translated into English, among them *A Finite Thinking* and *The Ground of the Image*, Nancy's *Au fond des images* was a major influence on Lalucq as she wrote *Fortino Sámano*. Lalucq's serial poem and Nancy's commentaries on each of the separate poems in the series together comprise the volume that they have coauthored and we have translated.

Nancy was impressed by Lalucq's first collection, *Couper les tiges* (Compac't, 2001), which was published to acclaim in France, and invited her to participate in a colloquium on the lyric at the Centre d'études poétiques (ENS) in Lyons. ENS describes their dialogue collected in *Fortino Sámano* as a work in three parts, "the poem, its duplication, and its overflowing," and its formal variations as transcending the division between poetry and philosophy. *Fortino Sámano (Les débordements du poème)* is an interdisciplinary dialogue among poetry, art, and philosophy, at once innovative and written with an eye to classic aesthetic tradition (most particularly, the history of the visual Image or icon).

We had not seen Lalucq for almost two years, when we had first met to discuss the translation. At that meeting, the conversation ranged dizzingly from the poetics of hybridity to Nancy's thinking on the function of the poetic image, and so, to the productive dialogue between poet and philosopher that became the collection we were hoping to translate. We left the café with Lalucq's and Nancy's permission to proceed, and now, nearly done with a revised draft, we were hoping to catch the poet who had disappeared into the demands of new motherhood and a post-crash workload as a librarian at the Fondation Nationale des Sciences Politiques in Paris.

Lalucq wrote *Fortino Sámano* after seeing an exhibit of photographs on the Mexican Revolution by Agustin Victor Casasola. Her series is a meditation on the single, extant photograph of Sámano, a Zapatista lieutenant and counterfeiter, which Casasola snapped as Sámano, smoking a last cigar, appeared to stare death nonchalantly in the face moments before his execution by firing squad (it was reported that he himself gave the order to fire). This photograph is not reproduced for the book but is, rather, "transmitted" into poetic images over the course of forty poems. Little is known about Sámano, and Lalucq's poem makes no attempt to be biographical or historical. Rather, she treats the image itself, the fact that the camera caught the image of life just prior to its end: what, then, does the image represent? is among the questions Lalucq poses.

Nancy's section, *Les débordements du poème*, is a series of poetic commentary on each of the poems in Lalucq's series. It is thus a philosophical contemplation of the specific poem, *Fortino Sámano*, and also of the poetic image: what does it do and how does it do it? Fascinating, full of punning wordplays, with exquisite attention to the lyric qualities of Lalucq's language, Nancy's section is itself a poetic investigation of the lyric genre, which works hand-in-hand with Lalucq's poems. Among the challenges of translating this work was addressing the issue of the relationship of the two parts. In the poem, Lalucq investigates how the photographic image resists poetic appropriation, just as Nancy explores how the poem resists philosophical explication. Nancy's section thus contemplates both the poem, *Fortino Sámano*, and Poetry. As ENS describes the project, "There's no schism between the two sections, but interaction. It's about a trans-mission, a trans-position or an exchange of knowledges." The two sections are distinct and intertwined.

The significant question for us was how to capture both the distinctiveness and the intertextuality of the two. Nancy's commentary is at once so precise and playful in response to Lalucq's language that, again and again, we revised the translation toward such precision of inquiry and language, with a necessarily fastidious attention to the language's lyric qualities – this despite the poem's dense textuality. This practice was, serendipitously, what Lalucq insisted upon when, at last, she arrived. We hadn't been sure we'd recognize her, but how could one mistake the woman approaching with a baby, a stroller, a diaper bag, and a backpack of books? And amid ministrations to her toddler, she listened patiently to our questions as we had the opportunity to confer with her in person one more time.

Virginie Lalucq

FORTINO SÁMANO

VIRGINIE LALUCQ

FORTINO SÁMANO

Jakobson dit que l'aphasie mange la langue à l'envers de son acquisition. Les articulations les plus récentes partent les premières.

Une bouche qui se défait commence par les lèvres.

J'ai pensé la même chose du vers. Les règles du vers disparaissent une à une dans sa destruction, selon un ordre, lui aussi, aphasique. Comme si les poètes défaisaient leur bâtiment étage par étage.

JACQUES ROUBAUD, *Quelque chose noir*

Jakobson says that aphasia devours language in reverse order to its acquisition. The most recent articulations going first.

A mouth coming undone starts at the lips.

I've held the same about verse. In the course of its destruction, rules of versification drop one by one in, likewise, aphasic order. As though the poets dismantled their house floor by floor.

JACQUES ROUBAUD, *Some thing black*
(trans. Rosmarie Waldrop)

Combien mes bourreaux étaient-ils / charmants ? /
L'image ne dit rien du règlement de comptes /
central / de la fusillade / et du léger liséré de
sang / qui s'ensuivra / pour l'instant / je souris /
pour l'instant / mon casier judiciaire / se vide / et
encore / sans lasso

How many of my executioners were / charming? /
The image tells us nothing about settling scores /
central / to this shooting / or of the light brim of
blood / that follows / at the moment / I'm smiling /
at the moment / my criminal record / empties /
and there's no / lasso yet

Si l'exécution / fut / sommaire / ou non /
le mur a des allures de figurant / derrière /
au premier plan / l'image n'est pas un stétho-
scope / pas plus / que je ne suis   un héros /
ou un acteur de cinéma / l'image ne dit pas /
si mon rythme cardiaque / s'accélérera / à cet
instant précis / je souris largement / je suis fort /
je suis le pire salaud qui soit / je me fusille /
je fume / mon dernier cigare / après quoi me
relève / et vous souris encore /

Whether the execution / was / summary / or not /
the wall's an alluring extra / in the background /
in the foreground / the image is not a stetho-
scope / any more / than I am / a hero / or
movie actor / the image does not say /
whether my heartbeat / speeds up / at this
very instant / I'm grinning wide / I am strong /
the worst son of a bitch alive / I'll shoot myself /
smoke / my last cigar / after which I'll rise /
to grin at you again /

Nuit centrale. Trou noir. Est-ce que je peux
est-ce que je vais photographier cela ? Le long
déroulé d'encre du mot. Déhanché.
Dans le métro, position assise de la main
de la petite fille qui observe le geste du
trompettiste. Position debout. Nonchalance
du déhanché. Pression des humeurs. Le poème
est mental. Son écriture physique. Nonchalance
du déhanché. Pression des humeurs. Et
que ça gicle, déborde partout.
Est-ce que je peux est-ce que je vais photogra-
phier cela, les débordements du poème ? La
pression est forte. Samanesque. Ou bien son
centre.

Middle of night. Black hole. Can I
should I photograph that? The long
unwound ink of words. Asway.
In the metro, the hand at rest of
the little girl watching the trumpeter
play. Who's standing. A nonchalant
sway. Pressure of moods. The poem
is cerebral. Its writing physical. A
nonchalant sway. Pressure of moods.
Let it spurt, flow all over
everywhere. Can I should I photograph
this, the overflowing of the poem? The
pressure is strong. Samanesque. Even its
center.

Au début, je n'ai pas bien saisi : il me semblait qu'une courte phrase aurait pu, aurait dû suffire, suffire mais rien n'est suffisant : le négatif est sous-exposé. Le temps que je comprenne qu'il me faudrait photographier dans l'obscurité – ce, sans flash – et la lumière s'était déplacée.

In the beginning, I didn't know: it seemed
to me a short phrase could do, ought to do,
to suffice, but nothing suffices: the negative
is under-exposed. In the time it took me to
understand that I had to photograph in dark-
ness – that's, with no flash – the light had
moved.

De toute façon / le mur progresse en pointillé /
je n'y échapperai pas / ses briques / en poin-
tillé / je n'aurai qu'à donner l'ordre / de tirer /
et les forces fédérales / s'exécuteront / avant
même que la fumée épaisse / de mon cigare /
ne vienne toucher le sol / sans s'éteindre /
cependant

Anyway / the wall is lined with dots /
I cannot escape / these bricks / of dot-
ted lines / I have only to give the order /
to fire / and federal troops / execute it /
before the thick smoke / from my cigar /
touches the ground / not gone out /
however

Et l'ombre était devenue Fortino et j'étais
l'ombre suivant son ombre suivant mon
ombre devenue Fortino.

And the shadow became Fortino and I was
the shadow following his shadow following
my shadow become Fortino.

Sans s'éteindre / cependant / si je contemple
à la loupe / les herbes potagères / ou les flo-
cons de neige / à l'instant / les fenêtres / se
couvrent / de fleurs de gel /

Not gone out / however / if I contemplate
under the lens / blades of grass / or snow-
flakes / in that moment / the window /
flowers / with frost /

Voulez-vous savoir autre chose ?

Eh bien, si je passe tout mon temps à écrire des mots, parfois très compliqués, avec des morceaux de glace, c'est que j'aime jouer au jeu de la raison froide.

Want to know something else?

All right, if I spend all my time writing
words, at times very intricate ones, with
pieces of ice, it's because I love to play
a game of cold reason.

Commence par les lèvres / ne t'arrête pas /
syllabe / après / syllable / reprends / STOP /
FOR-TI-NO / STOP /

Reprends / lettre / par lettre / ne t'arrête pas /
ta langue / claquera / contre / ton palais /
STOP / reprends / SÁ-MA-NO / STOP / reprends /
je ne te lâcherai / pas / STOP / tu parleras /
parlerai-je / STOP / nous / nous / parlerons /
ensemble / il y aura / parole / STOP / te stop-
perai-je /

Ta langue / arrivera / étrangère / impossible /
balbutiante / douloureuse / cependant / je te
comprendrai / tu t'étonneras / tu me feras /
le rapport / de ton étonnement / j'essaierai /
de te traduire / du français au français / je
n'y arriverai pas / j'aurai / la bouche / défai-
te / paralysée / gelée / je / tu / nous nous en
voudrions /

Begin with the lips / do not stop there /
syllable / after / syllable / again / STOP /
FOR-TI-NO / STOP /

Again / letter / by letter / don't stop /
Language / clicks / against / your palate /
STOP / again / SÁ-MA-NO / STOP / again /
I won't leave you / alone / STOP / you'll
speak / I'll speak / STOP / we'll / both /
speak / at once / have / words / STOP /
I'll stop you /

Your language / grows / strange / painful /
stuttering / impossible / however / if I
understand you / you'll be astonished /
and tell me / you're astonished / I'll try /
to translate you / from French to French /
if I fail / my mouth / will freeze / un-
done / paralyzed / I / you / we would hate
ourselves /

/ STOP / je te stopperai / à l'envers / mangerai /
ma langue / je te ferai / parler / STOP / comme
d'autres / font / chanter / je ne te lâcherai /
pas / STOP / étage / par / étage / palais dur /
après / voile / STOP / je te ferai parler /

i / ę / ę / a / ü / oę / ő / u / ǫ / ų / â : répète /
après moi /

/ STOP / I'll stop you / and in reverse / devour /
language / I'll make you / speak / STOP / as
others / make one / sing / I won't leave you /
alone / STOP / floor / by / floor / hard palate /
after / soft / STOP / I will make you speak /

i / ę / ę / a / ü / œ / ő / u / ǫ / ų / â: repeat /
after me /

Unblindfolded / j'ai tout silencé / cigare en
bouche / c'est dans le silencing / que j'ai
trouvé un mécanisme de défense / afin qu'ils
n'introduisent pas leur patrimoine génétique /
dans mes chromosomes / un rictus / plutôt /
je ne souris pas / je m'embrasse / jusqu'à tant
qu'un froid glacial / me pénètre / vous
pénètre / jusqu'au cœur /
(les signaux chimiques / qui circulent en moi /
et que vous pouvez voir à l'œil nu / sont
capables de s'éteindre / comme tout gène /
artificiellement introduit)

Unblindfolded / I've silenced everything /
cigar in mouth / it's in the silencing / I've
found a defense mechanism / so that they
can never introduce their genetic code /
into my chromosomes / a rictus / instead /
I do not smile / I hold myself / until a
glacial cold / penetrates me / penetrates
you / to the heart /
(the chemical signals / that circulate in me /
which you can see with the naked eye / are
capable of dying out / like all artificially /
introduced genes)

Sachant qu'elle est une falsification de la
devise, l'image change fatalement de signi-
fication. Fausse monnaie. Acte de guerre.
Tout dépend encore de quel côté de la lunette
on enregistre : question de focale, question
d'angle aussi. Ni viorne ni scabieuse, un mini-
mum de diablerie est nécessaire (s'impose) ou
ainsi (sinon) la légende disparaît. (L'enregis-
trement d'un désarroi puis d'une exécution
n'est pas celui d'un prisonnier politique.)

Given that the currency is counterfeit,
the meaning of the image changes irre-
vocably. False money. Act of war.
It all depends on which end of the lens
is used: question of focus, question of
angle also. Not viburnum or scabious,
a bit of devilry's necessary (essential)
or else (if not) the legend will vanish.
(Recording of a disarray then execution
which is not of a political prisoner.)

Dans le conte d'Andersen, les flocons de neige pareils à des abeilles blanches ont une reine, grande, belle et froide. Avant de retourner dans son royaume, La Reine des Neiges passe dans une des rues du conte et à l'instant les fenêtres se couvrent de fleurs de gel. Munie d'un traîneau à propulseur intégré de flocons neigeux et d'un grand manteau verglacé, La Reine des Neiges ne constitue pas vraiment un modèle de réchauffement (aussi, se blottir dans ses bras est un pari risqué contre la mort, sous peine de glaciation immédiate) et son régiment de flocons la protège en rangs serrés (hérissons blancs, ours rebondis, paquets de serpents : une armée de neige vivante, en somme). Son château constitué de poussières de neige n'a ni portes ni fenêtres. Au centre de cette forteresse aussi légère et volatile que la paille, un lac glacé faisant office de trône.

In the Andersen fairytale, snowflakes
hover like white bees around their
queen, tall, beautiful and cold. Before
returning to her realm, The Snow Queen
walks down one of the streets in the tale
and every window blooms with flowers
of frost. Riding a sled with internal
snowflake propulsion, swathed in a large,
black-iced cape, The Snow Queen's
never considered a model of warmth
(snuggling in her arms is a risky bet
with death, on pain of being frozen
in a flash). Her frosty regiments protect
her in tight ranks (white hedgehogs,
rotund bears, packs of snakes: in short,
an army of living snow). Her castle is
built of powdery snow with no doors no
windows. In the center of this fortress
as light and airy as chaff, a frozen lake
serves as her throne.

En fumant / les derniers instants / de mon cigare / en les confrontant / dans le même tissu de toile / avec des images à coupe automatique / c'est-à-dire sans signification délibérée / mais froidement glaciales / / j'avance mon armée / (Tous sont flocons de neige vivants) / (un éclat dans l'œil et voilà le cœur piqué / le cœur pareil à un bloc de glace / j'avance / en belligérante vitalité / c'est à moi / de donner / le signal / de leur exécution /

By smoking / the last moments / of my
cigar / facing them / in the same canvas
clip / with images cut automatically /
which is to say with no deliberate meaning /
with glacial cold / / my army advances /
(All of it living snowflakes) / a splinter
in the eye and heart's pierced / the heart
is a block of ice / I advance / bellicosely
vibrant / It's me / who gives / the order /
they execute /

Neutralité : vous m'avez demandé d'être neutre,
pas étonnant que je neutralise tout, après.

Après / une certaine quantité / de mouvement /
nulle / pour ainsi dire / se déplace / avec moi / le
curseur / sans la légende / je suis dépossédée / se
déplace / et l'image / ne m'appartient plus / elle
est / pour ainsi dire / *como nullo* / pour ainsi dire /
un mouvement partagé / sans effet observable /
que je transporte avec moi /

Neutrality: you asked me to be neutral,
no surprise, after that, I neutralize everything.

After / a certain amount / of movement /
nothing / one might say / is displaced / with
me / the cursor / without the legend / I'm
dispossessed / displaced / the image / no longer
mine / it is / one might say / *como nullo* /
one might say / a movement shared / to no
observable effect / is what I bring with me

Un mouvement partagé par plusieurs corps
n'influe pas /
Prenez 1 dictateur + 1 dictateur / ça nous fait
2 dictateurs /
Ça nous fait un sous-titre et demi qui n'influe
pas /

A movement which several bodies share
impacts nothing /
Take 1 dictator + 1 dictator / that makes
2 dictators /
One and a half subheadings which impact
nothing /

Effet massicot de l'image.

The guillotined effect of the image.

J'affronte et je fuis. Tranchant de l'image : je vois du sang, me coupe, panse la plaie, sans perdre connaissance cette fois je le lèche bien en face droit dans les yeux injectés de Fortino, j'affronte je soutiens son regard, c'est un printemps Marnie loin-sous-les-bombes, un printemps digne de l'été et en cela presque obscène avec ses robes et ses jupes flambant neuf, ses mules, ses forsythias jaune d'or, ses dj volatiles. C'est un printemps qui perd son sang après un régime idéologique drastique et tu me demandes, tu insistes – comment ça va ?

I face it and flee. The image's sharp edge:
I see the blood, cut myself, dress the gash,
not losing consciousness this time I lick it
in front of the bloodshot eyes of Fortino,
I look him right in the eye, it's spring,
a Marnie remote-from-the-bombs spring
ready for summer, almost obscene with its
dresses and spanking new skirts, its mules,
its yellow-gold forsythias, ephemeral dj.
It's a spring that has lost so much blood
after an ideological drastic regime and
you ask me, you insist – how's it going?

– Je sais me mettre en rang

– Je n'oublie pas mon service

– Je lève le doigt pour parler

– Je ne pose pas de questions idiotes

– Je fais rarement des fautes de copie

– (J'ai toujours mon matériel sur moi)

- I know how to get in line
- I never forget my duty
- I raise my hand to speak
- I never ask dumb questions
- I rarely make typos
- (I always bring what I need)

D'où vient qu'il est absolument en mouvement et
absolument immobile en même temps ?

Est-ce parce qu'éloigné de son lieu, il cherche
absolument à y retourner ? Ou bien qu'il l'occupe
absolument ?

Un corps en mouvement laisse parfois des traces
dans les corps immobiles. D'où l'effet neigeux de
l'image : chaque chose à sa place est absolument
en mouvement est absolument au repos.

How can he be absolutely in motion and
absolutely motionless at the same time?
Is it because, far from his place, he seeks
absolutely to return there? Or to occupy it
absolutely?
A body in motion sometimes leaves traces
in motionless bodies. From which the snowy
image: each thing in its place is absolutely in
motion is absolutely at rest.

Un amour possiblement un amour pour les
baies de viorne et les scabieuses, ce bouquet

est absolument en mouvement

A love possibly a love for the berries of
virburnum and scabious, this bouquet

    is absolutely in motion

Hélices ou boucles flèches.   Faible distance.
En baladant une épaisseur par exemple – nous
échappe – nous proposons d'entrer en résis-
tance.   Une résistance de l'ordre de la taille
d'un cheveu après une division par 100 000.

Helixes or loops arrows. Short distance.
In toting around a thickness for example –
escapes us – we suggest joining in resis-
tance. A resistance on the order of a hair's
breadth after being divided by 100,000.

En une nanoseconde
une nanorésistance
nanoréfie l'espace-temps

In a nanosecond
a nanoresistance
nanoreifies space-time

me font simultanément l'effet d'un champ de
renoncules qui s'invite chez moi et que je
plastifie, faute d'y croire.

giving me simultaneously the impression of
a buttercup field inviting itself home with me
which I plastic-coat instead of believe in.

D'où vient qu'en le voyant nous ayons l'intui-
tion directe de la simultanéité ? D'où vient
que je suis là–je suis sous les bombes aient lieu
au même instant sur deux théâtres distincts ?
D'où vient cette voix, qui semble demander
« tout va bien » ?

When we see him, why do we feel the di-
rect intuition of simultaneity? Why when
I'm here – am I under bombs falling at
the same time on two separate stages?
Why this voice that seems to be asking,
"everything all right"?

Si, descendant de la rame du métro, l'aveugle
me dit « Attention, vous avez une marche », il
n'y aura pas la moindre once de condescen-
dance ni d'amertume dans sa voix. Juste une
certaine solidarité certaine. L'image ne dit
rien d'autre que cela : « Attention, vous avez
une marche » et je la rate, comme de bien
entendu, m'affale puis rebondis sur le sol ;
blessée, non, légèrement – c'est-à-dire à vie –
j'écris une lance dans chaque jambe : une
plaque s'est détachée.

If, as I exit a subway car, the blind man
calls to me, "Watch out! There's a step,"
he won't have one ounce of condescension
or bitterness in his voice. Just a certain
assertion of solidarity. The image says
nothing besides this: "Watch out! There's
a step" but I miss it, naturally, and fall
down then jump back up on the platform;
hurt, no, slightly – what I mean is for life –
I write with a lance in each leg: a patch
scraped off.

Lunette d'approche / je vois le peloton d'exé-
cution / mais je ne vois pas mon ombre / Es
ist die Rede (*erste Erinnerung*) / c'est l'histoire /
j'ai perdu mon image / Que nul ne boive plus
cette eau ou en pierre se changera

Telescopic lens / I can see the firing
squad / but not my shadow / Es ist die
Rede (*erste Erinnerung*) / In this story /
I lost my image / Let no one drink the
water lest he be turned to stone

Faites encore une fois l'essai de votre ombre /

D'un fil je me découvre / mais c'est vous qui dis-
paraissez /
Tué / je vous tue / seul tutoiement possible / mon
effigie reste / quand rien de vous n'est visible /

Try one more time with your shadow /

I pick off one thread / but it's you who dis-
appear /
Killed / I kill you / can only call you close /
my effigy remains / but nothing of you does /

Trois tours de muscle. Je suis en prison. Rien à se mettre sous la dent à la bibliothèque carcérale. J'y vais pourtant de mes suggestions d'achat. Bibliothèque vide, j'obtiens cependant l'adresse d'un éditeur, puis deux, puis trois. J'écris aux auteurs. « Qu'avez-vous fait ? » me demande-t-on. Je suis tous coupables et doublement puni : ne pouvant lire, je ne lis plus : donc, j'écris puis me lis. Tous coupables.

Three turns for the muscles. I'm in jail.
Nothing in the prison library to sink my
teeth into. I go there with my helpful
suggestions of books to buy. Library
empty, I find a publisher's address, then
a second, and a third. I write the authors.
"What did you do?" I'm asked. All guilty,
I'm doubly punished: forbidden to read,
I can't read: so I write then read myself.
All guilty.

avril je ne savais pas, mai j'appris, juin je notais

April I did not know, May I was learning, June I took note

Les mots qui te reviennent les revenants avec les injures les premières
phrases formées forment une langue ta langue *unelangue* revenant elle
revient aux mots

Words come back to you like ghosts with their insults the first formed
sentences forming a language your language *onelanguage* which
returning returns you to words

Je ne sais pas comment faire. Comment tu fais,
toi ? Comment la poser ma langue, dis ? Ma
langue aphasique ? Comment ?
Je parle et je n'ai plus d'image mentale du mot ; je
lis et il me faudrait des images, un livre illustré
pour chaque mot ; j'écris, ma tête est comme un
puzzle et je ne sais plus ranger : pour « huit » JE
dit « rouge », pour « cinq » JE dit « vert ».
Comment je fais ? Eh bien, c'est simple, je scanne
ce sentiment puis je le retravaille jusqu'à ce que
toute trace disparaisse.

I don't know how it's done. How do you
do that? How do you put that in language?
My aphasic language? How?
I speak but have no mental images for words
anymore; I read but need pictures from an
illustrated book for each word; I write
but my head is a puzzle and I don't know
how things go anymore: for "eight" **I** say
"red," for "five" **I** say "green."
What can I do? It's really quite simple, I scan
this feeling then work it through until every
trace disappears.

Comment font les gens ? Comment je fais ?
J'articule je rééduque je re- du début à la fin
prends le chemin à l'envers de son acquisi-
tion, j'essaie de me souvenir avec mes lèvres,
avec mes joues, avec ma langue puis avec mon
larynx puis avec mon pharynx quand ma tête
ne suit plus ; j'assemble les phonèmes dans
ma bouche si je ne peux plus articuler dans
ma tête <u>silencieusement</u>.
<u>Silencieusement</u>, je ne produis rien d'autre
que du silence, aussi mâcher les mots me fait
du bien.

How have people done it? How do I?
I enunciate, I rehab, I re- from start to
finish take the route of acquisition in
reverse, try to remember with my lips,
my cheeks, my tongue then with my
larynx then my pharynx when my head
won't follow; I assemble the phonemes
in my mouth if I can no longer enunciate
them in my head <u>silently</u>.
<u>Silently</u>, I produce nothing other than
silence, so chewing words does me
some good.

Je peux longer le mur, je peux compter les
briques, je peux. Je peux me demander combien
de temps ça prendra, je peux me dire que ça
prendra le temps que ça prendra, je peux me dire
que ce temps est bien long mais qu'il est court
aussi. Je peux.

I can slide along the wall, I can count the bricks, I can. I can ask myself how much time this will take, I can tell myself that this will take the time it takes, I can tell myself that this time is long enough but it's also short. I can.

Ici une épithète se détache * cette étoile est
pourtant bien polaire (*her polartime* : un refrain
entêtant s'échappe d'un poème de Dickinson)
et *les vertes prairies font mes noires pensées*
comme si tout adjectif était en soi une épithète
de nature, une redondance et que nous ne
faisions rien d'autre que cela : donner les
définitions des mots que nous plaçons sur la
page, déclinaisons à l'infini.

Here an epithet comes loose * this star
is in fact polar (*her polartime*: a persistent
refrain escapes from a Dickinson poem)
green meadows make my thoughts black
as if any adjective in itself were an epithet
by nature, a redundancy, so that we do
nothing else besides this: give definitions
for the words we place on the page,
declensions to infinity.

Depuis je conjugue, activement je décline – IT
MAY BE WINTER OUTSIDE (BUT IN MY HEART IT'S
SPRING) aussi pauciflorement que possible – les
refrains sont autant de téguments
Enveloppes enveloppes légères je m'enveloppe
when
the temperature dips
langs langsam
trois degrés plus bas
le texte est neigeux fait-il froid
peut-être congèle-t-il à vue d'œil

Because I conjugate, I actively decline – IT
MAY BE WINTER OUTSIDE (BUT IN MY HEART
IT'S SPRING) as paucifloral as possible – the
refrains are all integuments
Envelopes light envelopes I envelop myself in
when
the temperature dips
langs langsam
three degrees lower
the page is snowy it is cold
perhaps it's freezing before our eyes

N'importe je re-
sample du Barry White
frain dans le texte c'est la chute.

Whatever I re-
sample of the Barry White
frain is where the text falls.

Longer le mur, compter les briques. Se demander combien de temps ça prendra. Se dire que ça prendra le temps que ça prendra.

Slide along the wall, count the bricks. Ask yourself how much time it will take. Tell yourself that it will take the time it takes.

La lune, c'est du planétaire, tu l'as bien noté.
Les talus, on leur enlève les barbes à l'aide d'une
faucille, ça s'appelle *barbeyer* ou *disac'her*, j'ai
bien noté que je disac'he depuis des semaines je
barbeye

Herbes après haies fossés feuille forme tige

Pourtant

les mots ne sont pas des étiquettes d'espèce (elles
doivent être en papier blanc ordinaire, collé et un
peu résistant sans être épais) puisque les mots ne
sont pas suffisants (ils ne permettent pas de placer
tous les renseignements nécessaires). Par exemple,
un mot de 0,38 m de long sur 4 à 5 de hauteur ne
suffit pas pour les contenir. Autant que possible,
les mots ne sont pas tous semblables, c'est ce qui
les différencie des étiquettes (les étiquettes ont
intérêt, elles, à être identiques pour les besoins de
l'échantillonnage).

The moon, you have noticed its planetariness.
The embankments, someone trimmed their beards
with a scythe, call it *to pare down* or *skive
off*, I've noticed I skive off that for weeks I
pare down

Grass then hedge ditch leaf form stem

Yet

words are not a kind of label (those
should be on plain white paper, glued and
a bit sturdy without being too thick) since
words are not enough (they don't allow us
to put in all the necessary pieces of information).
For example, a word 0.38 yards long and 4 to 5
yards high is not large enough to contain them.
As much as possible, words are not all alike,
this is how they differ from labels (it's in the
nature of labels to be identical to meet the needs
of sampling).

JEAN-LUC NANCY

LES DÉBORDEMENTS
DU POÈME

JEAN-LUC NANCY

THE OVERFLOWING OF
THE POEM

Fortino Sámano

Commence la lecture. Au titre, par le titre, comme il se doit. Le titre est un nom propre. Il ne m'annonce pas s'il intitule un récit fictif, une biographie, un essai ou un poème. Ce dernier genre serait le moins probable, si je ne savais déjà que je lis un poème. On devrait s'arrêter là-dessus : sur les préalables que toute lecture comporte dans un savoir antérieur relatif au genre du livre ou aux raisons qu'on a de le lire. Mais laissons cela ici. La lecture a déjà été débordée : avec ou sans savoir du genre, j'entends du chant dans ce nom. Il rime avec lui-même, il double une cadence à trois temps, il rend un son latin et enfin il paraît glisser des allusions à la fortune ou à la force, à la main, au « mano a mano » ou bien à quelque shaman. Mais en même temps il dérobe tout sens, et le dérobe deux fois au moins : une fois à l'instar de tout nom propre, une autre fois en tant que titre qui laisse ignorer s'il désigne plutôt un homme ou plutôt le texte qui vient, dont il est la venue.

FORTINO SÁMANO

Begin reading. At the title, with the title, as one does. The title is a name. It doesn't tell me if it is a title for a novel, a biography, an essay or a poem. This last genre I would think the least likely, except that I know I am reading a poem. This gives me pause: the act of reading any book involves prior knowledge of its genre and reasons for reading it. But let's move on. The reading has already overflowed: with or without knowing the genre, I hear a song in this name. It rhymes with itself, it doubles a cadence of three beats, it strikes a latinate note, and at last points to fortune or force, at hand, from "hand to hand," or perhaps to some shaman. But at the same time the name hides its meaning, hides it in at least two ways: first as itself, like all names, and second as a title that obscures whether it refers to a man or to the following text, which comes now.

Jakobson dit que l'aphasie mange la langue à l'envers de son acquisition. Les articulations les plus récentes partent les premières.

Une bouche qui se défait commence par les lèvres.

J'ai pensé la même chose du vers. Les règles du vers disparaissent une à une dans sa destruction, selon un ordre, lui aussi, aphasique. Comme si les poètes défaisaient leur bâtiment étage par étage.

JACQUES ROUBAUD, *Quelque chose noir*

Il vient une épigraphe. D'un autre poète et qui parle du vers. Me laisse attendre une aphasie, et une disparition ordonnée du vers. Mais je comprends qu'il reste au moins « le vers », et de lui la règle la plus ancienne, l'étage le plus archaïque (un sous-sol ? une cave ? une fondation ?). Je pense : Virginie veut me conduire au fond du vers. Comment le philosophe peut-il lire le poème ? En allant au fond. Mais le philosophe ne connaît que les fondements – sait-il quelque chose du fond, des fonds en général ?

Jakobson says that aphasia devours language in reverse order to its acquisition. The most recent articulations going first.

A mouth coming undone starts at the lips.

I've held the same about verse. In the course of its destruction, rules of versification drop one by one in, likewise, aphasic order. As though the poets dismantled their house floor by floor.

JACQUES ROUBAUD, *Some thing black*
(trans. Rosmarie Waldrop)

Here is the epigraph. By another poet speaking of verse. I am left waiting for aphasia, and for an orderly disappearance of verse. But I understand that at least "versification" remains, and with it the oldest rule, the most archaic floor (a basement? a cave? a foundation?). I think: Virginie wants to lead me to the ground of verse. How can the philosopher read the poem? By going to that ground. But the philosopher knows only about the fundamentals – does he know the ground of anything, of grounds in general?

Combien mes bourreaux étaient-ils / charmants ? /
[. . .]

    Le texte commence : mais où commence-t-il ? Ou bien à partir d'où ? Si je laisse l'épigraphe dans son suspens liminaire, que ferai-je du titre ? N'a-t-il pas déjà commandé l'ouverture entière du poème ? Et si ce titre est un nom propre, ne se trouve-t-il pas en position du nom d'un personnage de théâtre : le vers qui suit, le premier vers, serait donc sa parole, en première personne (« mes bourreaux »). Tout le poème est-il la parole de Fortino Sámano ? C'est possible, c'est certain. Le poème est toujours en première personne, que cela soit inscrit ou non par la grammaire. Avant toute chose, le poème parle en son nom propre : il est la langue en première personne. Et qui parle de ses bourreaux : ceux qui la charment, ceux qui la fusillent du regard, ceux qui lui font courir son plus grand risque et son unique chance.

    Fortino parle de ses bourreaux : combien étaient-ils ? Il ne le sait plus, ou bien à quel point étaient-ils charmants ? Une barre oblique sépare les deux possibilités de lecture. Je compte cette coupe (convenons de nommer « coupe » chaque fragment découpé par des barres obliques) comme – disons, un demi-vers, une décomposition ou une déconstruction du vers qui redonne du vers en chaque morceau. « Charmants », détaché, s'entend à la fois lié et séparé. Bourreaux charmants, et « charmants » comme adressé aux lecteurs dont je suis. Pourquoi serions-nous charmants sinon parce que suscitant le charme : notre lecture ouvre le chant et la magie du carmen, *des* carmina. *Bourreaux, donc, les charmes ? Oui, s'ils supplicient la parole pour la faire* verser : *tourner et tomber, d'étage en étage jusqu'au plus bas, au plus profond.*

How many of my executioners were / charming? /
[. . .]

The text begins: but where does it start? Or where is it
beginning? If I leave the epigraph suspended in the opening, what should
I do with the title? Isn't it already commanding the whole opening of
the poem? And if this title is a name, isn't it to be taken as the name of
a dramatic character: the line that follows, the first line, should be his
speech, in first person ("my executioners"). Is the whole poem the speech of
Fortino Sámano? It's possible, certainly. The poem is always in the first
person, whether inscribed in the grammar or not. Above all, the poem
speaks in its own name: it is language in the first person. And who speaks
of his executioners: those who charm the first person, the ones who look
daggers, the ones who make the first person run the greatest risk and take
the only chance.

Fortino speaks of his executioners: how many were there?
He doesn't know anymore, or whether they were charming? A slash
separates the two possible readings. I consider this cut (convenient to
call a "cut" each fragment cut off by the slash) as – let's say, a half-line, a
decomposition or deconstruction of the line that makes a line of each small
piece. "Charming," detached, can be read as both connected and separate.
Charming executioners, and "charming," as an address to readers among
whom I am one. How would we be charming without having invoked
charms: our reading opens to the chant and magic of carmen, the carmina.
Executioners, then, of charms? Yes, if they render speech to make it spill: to
turn and to fall, floor by floor, down to the very bottom, the deepest depths.

[...] L'image ne dit rien du règlement de comptes /
central / de la fusillade / et du léger liséré de
sang / qui s'ensuivra / pour l'instant / je souris /
pour l'instant / mon casier judiciaire / se vide / et
encore / sans lasso

*Quelle image ? A-t-on vu une image ? Virginie m'a dit qu'il n'y
aurait pas, dans son livre, la photographie de Fortino Sámano devant son
peloton d'exécution. Je n'aurai donc pas vu d'image. Or elle ne dit rien. Je
m'avise que cela se dit dans un alexandrin : « L'image ne dit rien du règlement
de comptes » – tout de suite, déjà, le vers cardinal du poème français. Ce n'est
pas un hasard. C'est pourquoi la coupe suivante dit lapidairement « central ».*
    *L'image ne dit rien : or l'image est par excellence qualité poétique.
L'image, c'est le poème. L'image absente, c'est le poème qui fait image en
parlant : ainsi « léger liséré de sang » se voit en se lisant, en se disant, se
voit littéralement allitéré dans un filet rouge soigneusement brodé. Virginie
choisit l'orthographe avec deux accents aigus plutôt que « liseré » pour
insister sur la minceur figée du filet carmin qui s'ensuivra. Juste avant
qu'il soit versé, « pour l'instant / je souris / pour l'instant ». Je souris
maintenant en vue de cet instant. Je souris à l'instant et pour qu'il reste
cet instant. Je souris à son éternel retour. Un sourire à la mort légère qui
ne dure qu'un instant, un sourire à l'immobilité du moment où ça verse : le
sens suspendu dans une imminence qui restera imminente. Le sens n'aura
pas lieu. L'image ne dit rien. Voilà le poème : sur le bord, en lisière, en liséré.
Et cela ne fait pas un lasso : pas une boucle qui entrave, pas plus que Fortino
n'est attaché devant ses fusilleurs. Son sang et ses manquements à la loi se
vident librement. Pourtant je ne peux pas ne pas entendre comment le sang
se reprend dans le sans lasso : le filet carmin fait aussi boucle où se prend le
sens ainsi captif de l'instant qui n'aboutira jamais.*

[. . .] The image tells us nothing about settling scores /
central / to this shooting / or of the light brim of
blood / that follows / at the moment / I'm smiling /
at the moment / my criminal record / empties /
and there's no / lasso yet

What image? Did anyone see an image? Virginie told me there won't be a photograph in her book of Fortino Sámano in front of the firing squad. Then I won't have seen an image. But it says nothing. I notice that this is said in an alexandrine: "The image tells us nothing about settling scores" – right away, already, the cardinal line of French poetry. It is not by accident. It is why the cut that follows says concisely "central."

The image says nothing: but the image has par excellence a quality of the poetic. Absent the image, the poem will make an image in speaking: just as "light brim of blood" is seen when read, when said to oneself, seen literally alliterated in the carefully elaborated welling of red. Virginie chooses wording that doubles blood's plosive, insisting on the coagulating, carmine trickle to follow. Just before it is to spill, "at the moment / I'm smiling / at the moment." I smile now having this moment in mind. I smile at this moment so that it will remain this moment. I smile thinking of its eternal return. A smile for an easy death lasting only an instant, a smile for the stillness of the moment before it spills: the meaning suspended in an imminence which remains imminent. The meaning never occurs. The image says nothing. Here's the poem: on the rim, the edge, on the brim. This does not make a lasso: not a loop that would fetter, any more than Fortino is, tied in front of his killers. His blood and his crimes empty out freely. But I cannot not hear how the blood is caught by this no-lasso: the trickle of carmine makes a loop where meaning is captured by a moment that will never come to anything.

Si l'exécution / fut / sommaire / ou non /
le mur a des allures de figurant / derrière /
au premier plan / l'image n'est pas un stétho-
scope / pas plus / que je ne suis / un héros /
ou un acteur de cinéma / l'image ne dit pas /
si mon rythme cardiaque / s'accélérera / à cet
instant précis / je souris largement / je suis fort /
je suis le pire salaud qui soit / je me fusille /
je fume / mon dernier cigare / après quoi me
relève / et vous souris encore /

Il est mort il se relève, ressuscité si l'on veut ou bien imagé pleinement, passé dans ce silence de l'image sans cœur qui bat et sans déclaration sur celui qui parle sinon qu'il parle et qu'il prononce cet instant précis où il tombe et se relève – comme un vers, de nouveau, chute, coupe et revers. L'exécution : tout est là, la mise en œuvre, la réalisation menée à terme. C'est pourquoi ce bloc est ouvert par un décasyllabe très cadencé avec rime interne à l'hémistiche : « Si l'exécution fut sommaire ou non. » Il y a dans le vers une exécution toujours en quelque façon sommaire du cours du sens, du discours qui ne se tient pas à l'instant. La coupe du cours, au contraire, n'a lieu qu'à l'instant précis : le sens s'y fusille lui-même – quel mot glacé, crépitant, sans appel – et la fumée du cigare, ici, qui monte encore mêlée à celle des fusils. Un poème est toujours, à chaque instant, un dernier mot sans conclusion.

Whether the execution / was / summary / or not /
the wall's an alluring extra / in the background /
in the foreground / the image is not a stetho-
scope / any more / than I am / a hero / or
movie actor / the image does not say /
whether my heartbeat / speeds up / at this
very instant / I'm grinning wide / I am strong /
the worst son of a bitch alive / I'll shoot myself /
smoke / my last cigar / after which I'll rise /
to grin at you again /

He's dead he gets up, resuscitated, if you like, or fully imagined, passing into the silence of this image with no beating heart, without clarifying who is speaking except that someone is speaking, someone announces the exact moment that he falls and gets up – like a line, anew, falling, cutting, reversing. The execution: everything is there, set into play, brought to term. That is why the verse opens with such a cadenced decasyllable and internal rhyme in the hemistich: "Whether the execution was summary or not." There is in the line an execution that is always in some sense summary, of the course of meaning, of discourse that does not relate to the moment. The break in that course, in contrast, must take place only at the precise moment: meaning shoots itself – what a cold word, sputtering, without appeal – and the rising smoke from the cigar, here, mixes with smoke from the guns. A poem is always, at each moment, a last word with no conclusion.

Nuit centrale. Trou noir. Est-ce que je peux
est-ce que je vais photographier cela ? Le long
déroulé d'encre du mot. Déhanché.
Dans le métro, position assise de la main
de la petite fille qui observe le geste du
trompettiste. Position debout. Nonchalance
du déhanché. Pression des humeurs. Le poème
est mental. Son écriture physique. Nonchalance
du déhanché. Pression des humeurs. Et
que ça gicle, déborde partout.
Est-ce que je peux est-ce que je vais photogra-
phier cela, les débordements du poème ? La
pression est forte. Samanesque. Ou bien son
centre.

Soudain les barres obliques ont disparu. A disparu le marquage
des fractions, fractures, fragmentations du texte. La notation de syncopes,
de coupes, d'apnées ou de haut-le-cœur. Pourquoi ? il ne sera sans doute pas
facile de répondre. Tout se passe ici comme s'il y avait passage au discours qui
serait celui de qui écrit, non du supposé Sámano face au peloton. Pourtant
« Nuit centrale. Trou noir » n'est pas moins syncopé. C'est même, ou bien
c'est en outre, la désignation de la syncope même : la nuit, le noir au milieu
du sens. Cela qui fait cadence. Ici notée comme nonchalance du déhanché.
C'est la pose de Sámano, c'est la pression d'une insolence devant la mort,
liée à la pression de la question posée le doigt sur la gâchette, pardon, sur
le déclencheur de l'appareil : photographier cela, est-ce possible, cela aura-
t-il lieu ? Le mot, le déhanché, la giclée et le débordement du poème font
une même chose. Une chose qui est au centre et qui en déborde, un excès
central du noir physique (l'encre, le déroulé du mot) sur le poème mental
(l'idée, l'image, pas encore le mot). Le mot est physique : le mot est nature et
matière, ordre des places, déplacements et forces. Le mot fait pression. Il ne
va pas seulement droit devant dans le sens, mais il appuie sur ses flancs : il se
déhanche. Le poème est un déhanchement des mots.

Middle of night. Black hole. Can I
should I photograph that? The long
unwound ink of words. Asway.
In the metro, the hand at rest of
the little girl watching the trumpeter
play. Who's standing. A nonchalant
sway. Pressure of moods. The poem
is cerebral. Its writing physical. A
nonchalant sway. Pressure of moods.
Let it spurt, flow all over
everywhere. Can I should I photograph
this, the overflowing of the poem? The
pressure is strong. Samanesque. Even its
center.

Suddenly the slashes disappear. The marks of fractions, fractures,
fragmentations in the text disappear. The notation of syncopations, of cuts, of
breath caught, of heaves. Why? There's probably no easy answer. Everything
here suggests that there's been a change of speaker to the one writing, not
as supposed Sámano facing the firing squad. Yet "Middle of night. Black
hole" is no less syncopated. It even has, or has in addition, the designation
of syncopation itself: the night, the darkness in the middle of meaning. That
creates cadence. Here, described as a nonchalant sway. This is Sámano's
pose, the pressure of an insolence in the face of death, connected to the pressing
question posed by the finger on the trigger, I mean, on the camera's shutter
release: is it possible to photograph this, will it occur? The words, the swaying,
the spurting and the overflowing of the poem all do the same thing. A thing
which is central to the poem and which overflows it, a central excess of black
materiality (the ink that words unwound) on the cerebral poem (the idea, the
image, not yet word). Words are physical: words are nature and matter, order
of place, changing place and force. Words exert pressure. They go straight
ahead of meaning, pressing at its sides: they sway themselves. The poem is a
swaying of words.

Au début, je n'ai pas bien saisi : il me semblait qu'une courte phrase aurait pu, aurait dû suffire, suffire mais rien n'est suffisant : le négatif est sous-exposé. Le temps que je comprenne qu'il me faudrait photographier dans l'obscurité – ce, sans flash – et la lumière s'était déplacée.

Ce sans flash : ce sang flashe – voilà ce qui remplace la barre oblique, le slash comme on dit en langue computérisée. Ce qu'au début elle n'a pas saisi, elle finit par le saisir au plus vif, au centre et dans le noir, le sang qui flashe, c'est lui qui éclaire la scène et qui l'éclaire, elle, la photographe, la poésie.

Du poème comme photographie : le langage saisi par l'instant lumineux, les mots plongés dans une émulsion sensible, et la syncope du déclic.

Le langage saisi par l'obscurité et par la suffisance de rien (rien ne suffit et il suffit de rien) : saisi par la mort, pour tout dire. Mais précisément, il ne peut pas tout dire. Aucune courte phrase, pas même un seul mot. Pas de dernier mot. Le dernier mot, « la mort », lui-même reste sous-exposé. Et le poème se passe tout entier dans cette sous-exposition. Le poème procède de cette exécution.

In the beginning, I didn't know: it seemed
to me a short phrase could do, ought to do,
to suffice, but nothing suffices: the negative
is under-exposed. In the time it took me to
understand that I had to photograph in dark-
ness – that's, with no flash – the light had
moved.

*This no-flash: this blood flush – here's what replaces the oblique
stroke, the slash as we say in the language of computers. What she did not
grasp in the beginning, she grasped keenly by the end, at the center and in
the dark, the blood flushing out, this is what illuminates the scene, shines a
light on her, the photographer, poetry.*

*The poem like a photograph: language captured in the illumined
moment, words plunged into a sensitive emulsion, and the syncopation of the
click.*

*Language grasped by darkness and by nothing's sufficiency
(nothing can suffice and nothing suffices): grasped by death, to say
everything. But precisely, everything cannot be said. No short phrase, not
even a single word. Not a last word. The last word, "death," remains under-
exposed. The whole poem takes place in this under-exposure. The poem
proceeds from this execution.*

De toute façon / le mur progresse en pointillé /
je n'y échapperai pas / ses briques / en poin-
tillé / je n'aurai qu'à donner l'ordre / de tirer /
et les forces fédérales / s'exécuteront / avant
même que la fumée épaisse / de mon cigare /
ne vienne toucher le sol / sans s'éteindre /
cependant

Les forces s'exécuteront en exécutant, en m'exécutant. Tout se fait rafale, les briques du mur et les saccades de la phrase. Rafale et fumée qui persiste, montant du sol comme le sang coule sur sa poitrine. Mais « cependant » suspend la strophe : « ce pendant », ce mot qui reste pendant, suspendu sans suite, littéralement appendu à l'extrémité de la phrase saccadée, syncopée. Qu'est-ce qu'un pendant ? Cela qui fait pendant à autre chose, qui équilibre et qui forme une symétrie. Comme les pendants d'une oreille à l'autre, comme les pendentifs sur les décolletés. Un mot fait pendant à l'absence des mots.

Anyway / the wall is lined with dots /
I cannot escape / these bricks / of dot-
ted lines / I have only to give the order /
to fire / and federal troops / execute it /
before the thick smoke / from my cigar /
touches the ground / not gone out /
however

Troops enforce orders by executing them, by executing me. As if everything is bursting, the bricks in the wall and the starts in the sentence. Bursts and drifting smoke, rising from the ground as blood runs down the chest. But "however" suspends the strophe, is pending: "how ever," this word that hangs in suspense, suspended with nothing to follow it, literally appended to the end of the startled, syncopated sentence. What is pending? That which, left hanging in the balance, creates symmetry, like earrings hanging on one ear as well as the other, like a pendant on the breast. A word left hanging in the absence of words.

Et l'ombre était devenue Fortino et j'étais
l'ombre suivant son ombre suivant mon
ombre devenue Fortino.

*De la fumée à l'ombre : au contour déposé par la lumière sur le mur,
découpe légendaire de l'origine corinthienne de la peinture. Photographie,
peinture, et le mot « ombre » qui projette la sienne sur le nom propre, sur la
fuite du sens de sa fortune et de sa fortitude, une ombre sienne et mienne, ni
sienne ni mienne mais l'ombre même, l'ombre en soi, celle qui précède la clarté
pour lui permettre de se découper et de s'ouvrir.*

And the shadow became Fortino and I was
the shadow following his shadow following
my shadow become Fortino.

*From smoke to shadow: to the contour left by light on the wall,
the legendary outline of the Corinthian origins of painting. Photography,
painting, and the word "shadow" that projects its own shadow onto the name,
onto the flight of the meaning of its fortune and fortitude, a shadow both his
and mine, neither his nor mine but the shadow itself, the shadow in itself,
which precedes the clear light that allows it to stand out, to open wide.*

Sans s'éteindre / cependant / si je contemple
à la loupe / les herbes potagères / ou les flo-
cons de neige / à l'instant / les fenêtres / se
couvrent / de fleurs de gel /

Soudain c'est ailleurs, ce n'est plus l'exécution, c'est une scène
d'intérieur et d'observation – mais non, c'est la même : ici, elle regarde la
photographie ou bien les herbes et les flocons. Ce n'est qu'un cabinet d'optique,
une camera obscura où elle observe – et soudain ce qui se fait voir ici est un gel
préparé par ses assonances potagères et de neige. Qu'est-ce donc qui gèle, qui se
gélifie, quelle gélatine ou quelle glace ? Toujours une affaire d'image, la gelée
de la pellicule ou la glace du miroir.

Mais aussi, fleurs de gel recouvrant les fenêtres, c'est un gel de la
vision, c'est une glaciation : ce qu'il y a de froid dans l'image comme dans la
mort. Fortino Sámano est refroidi, comme on dit chez les bandits (et lui, il
en est un pour les troupes fédérales). Refroidi cependant que son cigare brûle
encore. La question de l'image est la question d'un gel tout comme l'ombre
est froide et comme tout se glace dans cette scène d'exécution sommaire et
de héros impassible et narquois. Je comprends le poème comme ces fenêtres
couvertes de fleurs de gel ; dès qu'il y a fleur, la poésie est citée à comparaître ;
et elle comparaît en tant qu'« image poétique », comme on aime à dire. Quoi
d'autre fait la poésie, sinon l'image ? Mais quoi d'autre fait l'image, sinon le
gel, la glace, le verre froid des loupes ou fenêtres ?

Rappelons-nous : l'image ne dit rien – c'est en ne disant rien qu'elle
se fait image, c'est en gelant sur elle la parole. C'est en photographiant le sang
séché du sens.

Not gone out / however / if I contemplate
under the lens / blades of grass / or snow-
flakes / in that moment / the window /
flowers / with frost /

*Suddenly it's elsewhere, it is not the execution anymore, it is a scene
of interiority and observation – but no, it's the same: here, she regards the
photograph and also the grass and snowflakes. It is only an optical chamber, a
camera obscura from where she is making her observations – and suddenly
what is made visible is a glazing of frost prepared for by the assonance of blade
and flake. What freezes then, what is glazed with frost, what frosty and what
icy? It is always about the image, the glaze on the film or a mirror's frosted
glass.*

*But also, flowers of frost cover the windows, this is a glazing-over of
vision, a glaciation: what is cold in the image as in death. Fortino Sámano has
been iced, as gangsters say (and he is one to the Feds). Iced while his cigar still
burns. The question of the image is the question of frost just as the shadow is
cold and just as everything freezes over in this scene of the summary execution
of an impassive, sardonic hero. I understand the poem as being like these
windows covered with frost flowers; as soon as there are flowers, poetry is taken
to court; and appears as a "poetic image," one might say. What else is poetry
making, if not an image? But what else is making the image, if not frost, ice,
the cold glass of a magnifying lens or of windows?*

*Remember: the image says nothing – it is in saying nothing that
it becomes an image, it is in speech freezing over it. It is in photographing the
dried blood of meaning.*

Voulez-vous savoir autre chose ?

Eh bien, si je passe tout mon temps à écrire
des mots, parfois très compliqués, avec des
morceaux de glace, c'est que j'aime jouer au
jeu de la raison froide.

*Et voici qu'elle s'adresse à nous et parle clairement en première
personne en son nom de poète ou du moins de scripteur de mots. Elle, en
personne, c'est Virginie Lalucq, son nom a précédé le titre, son nom a précédé
celui de Fortino Sámano, ombre devant une ombre, imagière ouvrant l'image
ou l'observant à la loupe. « Virginie Lalucq » est un nom très froid, aussi froid
qu'est brûlant celui de Fortino Sámano avec son cigare aux lèvres.*

*Virginie fixe et glace Fortino, puis elle vient nous dire ce que nous ne
demandions pas : sa raison d'écrire. Cependant il n'est pas certain que nous
ne l'ayons pas demandé, en silence. Ce qui s'appelle « poème » est une machine
destinée à susciter l'interrogation : pourquoi donc est-ce écrit ? Au lieu que tout
autre texte répond à une attente, le poème ne s'emploie qu'à susciter l'attente
de sa propre raison. Et il répond ici : « la raison froide ». C'est une tautologie.
La froideur n'est pas un attribut contingent de la raison, mais une qualité
d'essence. On dit, c'est un* topos, *« la froide raison ». Virginie inverse et fait
tomber l'épithète comme une chute imprévue, comme un accident final. Il y
aurait donc une raison chaude, et c'est elle qui est refroidie. Comme Fortino,
comme la braise de son cigare. De la fumée chaude à l'ombre froide se joue le
jeu du gel. La raison du poème est de glacer l'image et de geler le sens. Geler
ce qui brûle, c'est la raison nécessaire et suffisante. Le feu givré, le sens séché,
c'est la raison.*

*Après tout, la flamme et la glace brûlent l'une et l'autre, et la glace
peut-être retient, contient et maintient la brûlure du feu : le coup de fusil, le
sang, le cigare.*

Want to know something else?

All right, if I spend all my time writing
words, at times very intricate ones, with
pieces of ice, it's because I love to play
a game of cold reason.

Now she addresses us, clearly speaking in the first person in her own
name as a poet or at least as a writer of words. Virginie Lalucq in person,
whose name came before the title, came before Fortino Sámano's name, shadow
before a shadow, image-maker opening the image up or observing it through
a lens. "Virginie Lalucq" is a very cold name, as cold as the name of Fortino
Sámano – with his cigar between his lips – is burning.

Virginie sets and freezes Fortino, and then she comes and tells us
what we did not ask to know: her reason for writing. It is not clear, however,
that we never asked silently. What one calls a "poem" is a machine intended
to provoke the question: why was this written? While any other text responds
to expectations, the poem devotes itself to creating the expectation of its own
reason. And here is its answer: "cold reason." This is a tautology. Coldness is
not an attribute contingent on reason, but an essential quality. One might say
it is a topos: *"the coldness of reason." Virginie turns and drops the epithet in*
like an unexpected end, a final accident. There might be hot reason, and that
is what is being chilled down. Like Fortino, like the embers of his cigar. From
hot smoke to cold shadow the game of ice is played. The purpose of the poem
is to freeze the image and frost over its meaning. To freeze what burns is the
necessary and sufficient reason for the poem. The frozen fire, dried meaning,
this is the reason.

After all, both the flame and the ice are burning, and perhaps ice
can retain, contain and maintain the fire's flames: the gun shot, the blood, the
cigar.

Commence par les lèvres / ne t'arrête pas /
syllabe / après / syllabe / reprends / STOP /
FOR-TI-NO / STOP /

Reprends / lettre / par lettre / ne t'arrête pas /
ta langue / claquera / contre / ton palais /
STOP / reprends / SÁ-MA-NO / STOP / reprends /
je ne te lâcherai / pas / STOP / tu parleras /
parlerai-je / STOP / nous / nous / parlerons /
ensemble / il y aura / parole / STOP / te stop-
perai-je /

Ta langue / arrivera / étrangère / impossible /
balbutiante / douloureuse / cependant / je te
comprendrai / tu t'étonneras / tu me feras /
le rapport / de ton étonnement / j'essaierai /
de te traduire / du français au français / je
n'y arriverai pas / j'aurai / la bouche / défai-
te / paralysée / gelée / je / tu / nous nous en
voudrions /

Comment elle enchaîne, nous avons entendu. « Le jeu de la raison
froide » – « commence par les lèvres ». Le slash revient et claque plus qu'avant,
claque les lèvres et la langue qui claque à son tour « contre / ton palais ». La
langue ici claque d'un sens à l'autre de son mot. Qu'est-ce que claquer ?
Gifler, mourir aussi. C'est un son clair et froid, une seule syllabe audible.
Il s'agit des syllabes qui claquent l'une après l'autre, sans arrêt, toujours en
reprise. Le nom claque et la langue entière se syllabise, se décompose en unités
syncopées. Syllabe, syncope, langue claquée, gelée, parlant dans son claquement
même, parlant là où ça claque, là où se rompt le lien parlant.

Il faut savoir lire : « je / tu / nous nous en voudrions / » reprenons
donc : je, tu, nous, nous en vous – drions : comme un prion, un vibrion, et comme
nous rions soudain là où nous sommes déchirés, blessés, en mal de langue. Mais
aucun doute, il s'agit de nous en vous comme de la langue en soi.

Begin with the lips / do not stop there /
syllable / after / syllable / again / STOP /
FOR-TI-NO / STOP /

Again / letter / by letter / don't stop /
Language / clicks / against / your palate /
STOP / again / SÁ-MA-NO / STOP / again /
I won't leave you / alone / STOP / you'll
speak / I'll speak / STOP / we'll / both /
speak / at once / have / words / STOP /
I'll stop you /

Your language / grows / strange / painful /
stuttering / impossible / however / if I
understand you / you'll be astonished /
and tell me / you're astonished / I'll try /
to translate you / from French to French /
if I fail / my mouth / will freeze / un-
done / paralyzed / I / you / we would hate
ourselves /

    We have heard the link she creates. "The game of cold reason" –
"begins with the lips." The slash is back and clicks more than before, clicking
the lips and language in turn clicking its tongue "against / your palate." Here's
language clicking from one meaning of the word to the other. What is to click?
To hit it off, also to fit in. The sound is clear and cold, one audible syllable.
It has to do with syllables clicking one after the other, without stopping, again
and again. The name clicks and the whole language syllablizes, decomposing
itself in syncopated units. Syllable, syncopation, language clicking shut,
frozen, speaking from inside the click itself, speaking where it clicks, where
the spoken link breaks.

    You must read this: "I / you / we would hate / ourselves /" like this: I,
you, who are we to hate our – selves : like cells, bacillus, and silly with laughing
suddenly we're rent, wounded, longing for language. No doubt this is as much
about who we are as about language itself.

/ STOP / je te stopperai / à l'envers / mangerai /
ma langue / je te ferai / parler / STOP / comme
d'autres / font / chanter / je ne te lâcherai /
pas / STOP / étage / par / étage / palais dur /
après / voile / STOP / je te ferai parler /

i / ę / ę̃ / a / ü / oę̨/ / ő / u / ǫ / ų / à : répète /
après moi /

    *La langue en soi, en moi comme en toi, la langue de toi à moi, la
langue est* stoppée *comme un télégramme : c'est une émission saccadée de
traits, de phonèmes, de voix, de vocalises, c'est un jet spasmodique de bribes du
désir de dire, c'est une dévoration interne pour venir à s'externer, à parler au-
dehors sans cesser pourtant à chaque syllabe de se heurter au « palais dur »
qui, tout en même temps, se déconstruit « étage / par / étage » comme le poème
dégringole de ses propres échafaudages et en même temps donc durcit ainsi
toujours mieux ses silex qui l'écorchent (la langue, je veux dire) autant qu'ils
la délient. Et moi, ici, lisant Virginie, j'écris « je veux dire », mais qui « je » et
quel vouloir ? C'est elle qui me fait parler et qui – à la limite – m'empêche de
parler pour la commenter, car elle m'oblige à* répéter *après elle comme elle l'a
écrit, exactement et ainsi me* stoppant, *c'est-à-dire m'interdisant de tenir mon
discours d'exégèse puisqu'il faut en passer par cela qu'elle me fait parler. Elle,
la poésie.*

    Mais stopper, *c'est aussi cet homonyme qui signifie repriser,
raccommoder (estouper, mettre de l'étoupe). Elle me raccommode ma langue,
comme un bas, comme une chemise.*

    *Il me faut comprendre qu'en effet le poème – et voici en quoi il
déborde – fait plus parler qu'il ne parle lui-même. Un poème est ce qui se glisse
dans la gorge et dans la langue de son lecteur/auditeur et qui le fait parler, qui
lui prend les mâchoires, les lèvres et le larynx pour le manger du dedans. Un
poème qui ne fait que parler devant moi et à moi, sans me plier à le parler à
mon tour, celui-là n'a pas débordé et a raté son coup.*

/ STOP / I'll stop you / and in reverse / devour /
language / I'll make you / speak / STOP / as
others / make one / sing / I won't leave you /
alone / STOP / floor / by / floor / hard palate /
after / soft / STOP / I will make you speak /

i / ę / ę / a / ü / œ / ő / u / ǫ / ų / â: repeat /
after me /

Language itself, in you as in me, language from you to me,
language with stops *like a telegram: a halting transmission of strokes,*
phonemes, voices, vocalics, spasmodic stream of bits of the desire to speak,
it is an internal rage to externalize, to speak outside without stopping at
each syllable that collides with the "hard palate," which, at the same time,
deconstructs itself "floor / by / floor" like the poem tumbling down its own
scaffolding but then, at the same time, always sharpening the flint that
chips it (I want to say language) as much as shapes it. Here I am reading
Virginie, I write "I want to say," but who's "I" and what do "I" want? She
makes me speak and – in the end – prevents me from making comments,
because she forces me to repeat after her *exactly as she wrote it, and she*
does this to stop *me, which is to say to forbid me from delivering my*
exegesis, since there is no way around the fact that what makes me speak is
her. That is, poetry.

But stop *is also a homonym that means to stitch up, to patch (to*
staunch, to stay). She patches my language like a sock, like a shirt.

I must understand that, in effect, the poem – and this is why
it overflows – makes us speak more than it says. A poem glides onto the
tongue and down the throat of its readers/listeners and makes us speak,
takes hold of our jaws, lips, larynx and devours us from the inside out.
A poem that does nothing but speak in front of us and at us, without
forcing us in turn to speak, has not overflowed and has missed the
mark.

Je répète donc. Je répète après elle, ou bien je répète « après moi » ?

« Après moi, le déluge », voilà ce qui arrive à force de répéter « après moi » : voilà ce qui arrive par la langue ; le déluge de la langue arrive, les fleuves et les mers débordent, toute la terre est noyée ; lorsqu'on est embarqué dans la langue, il n'y a plus de terre ferme ; c'est une arche vers laquelle nulle colombe n'apporte un rameau d'olivier ; il n'y a pas d'apaisement ; le débordement est sans fin, et c'est pourquoi le poème ne nous lâche pas.

Ne nous lâchent pas ces voix, ces voyelles, ces vocalises, ces vocations, invocations, convocations. À quoi sommes-nous convoqués ? À répéter toute la langue, élément par élément, toute la langue voyellée et consonnée en face d'un silencement obstiné.

So I repeat. I repeat after her, or do I repeat "after me"?

"After me, the deluge," this is what happens in the end by repeating "after me": this is what happens with language; the deluge of language comes, rivers and seas overflow, the whole earth drowns; when we are brought on board language, there is no more terra firma; language is an ark to which no dove brings an olive branch; there is no relief from this endless flooding: the poem never lets go of us.

These voices never let go of us, these vowels, vocations, invocations, convocations. To what are we convened? To repeat the whole of language, element by element, the whole of language vowelled and consonanted in the face of an obstinate silencing.

Unblindfolded / j'ai tout silencé / cigare en
bouche / c'est dans le silencing / que j'ai
trouvé un mécanisme de défense / afin qu'ils
n'introduisent pas leur patrimoine génétique /
dans mes chromosomes / un rictus / plutôt /
je ne souris pas / je m'embrasse / jusqu'à tant
qu'un froid glacial / me pénètre / vous
pénètre / jusqu'au cœur /
(les signaux chimiques / qui circulent en moi /
et que vous pouvez voir à l'œil nu / sont
capables de s'éteindre / comme tout gène /
artificiellement introduit)

*Alors, retour sur image. L'exécuté les yeux non bandés a vu venir
la mort à lui de face et le silence qu'elle porte. Il fait ce verbe, silencer, et
ce gérondif anglais silencing qui opère dans cet état suspendu entre verbe et
substantif que l'on connaît au dancing ou au thinking comme au tossing.
Silencing, ce serait le performing du poème, rictus par où revient, comme il
peut, le sourire du mourant déjà tordu sur la face figée : émission de signaux
qui ne signalent que ce resserrement du froid. Non pas le grand silence profond
où se réserve une parole plus profonde. Mais la glaciation qui atteint le cœur
du langage aussi bien que le langage du cœur (cette facilité sera-t-elle excusée
par sa nécessité ?). Le gel du sens, une fois de plus. Et la morsure de ce gel
comme une embrassade de moi-même, comme une étreinte en moi qui vous
étreint à vous couper le sens avec le souffle.*

Unblindfolded / I've silenced everything /
cigar in mouth / it's in the silencing / I've
found a defense mechanism / so that they
can never introduce their genetic code /
into my chromosomes / a rictus / instead /
I do not smile / I hold myself / until a
glacial cold / penetrates me / penetrates
you / to the heart /
(the chemical signals / that circulate in me /
which you can see with the naked eye / are
capable of dying out / like all artificially /
introduced genes)

*Freeze frame on image. The condemned whose eyes are not
blindfolded has faced the coming death and the silence it brings. He makes
this verb,* to silence, *and this gerund in English* silencing *that operates
in a state of suspension between verb and noun which we also know from*
dancing *or* thinking *as well as from* tossing. Silencing *might be the poem
performing* itself, rictus *which, if it can, brings back the dying man's* smile
already contorting his rigid face: emission of signals *that signal nothing but
this tightening of cold's grip. Not the deep grandeur of a silence guarding a
deeper word. But a glacial cold that reaches the heart of language as well as
the language of the heart (will such facility be forgiven because of necessity?).
Meaning freezes over again. The bite of this frost is like holding myself, like a
grip inside me that grips you until it takes meaning away with your breath.*

Sachant qu'elle est une falsification de la
devise, l'image change fatalement de signi-
fication. Fausse monnaie. Acte de guerre.
Tout dépend encore de quel côté de la lunette
on enregistre : question de focale, question
d'angle aussi. Ni viorne ni scabieuse, un mini-
mum de diablerie est nécessaire (s'impose) ou
ainsi (sinon) la légende disparaît. (L'enregis-
trement d'un désarroi puis d'une exécution
n'est pas celui d'un prisonnier politique.)

Devise et légende *: chose dite et qui doit l'être, non pas pour être
signifiée mais pour donner un ton, un mouvement, une direction. Devise
et légende sont enregistrées : inscrites en exergue d'un blason ou d'une
illustration. Tout ce poème est écrit au-dessous ou à côté de la photographie
de Sámano qui va mourir exécuté. Exergue, cela qui n'est pas dans l'œuvre.
L'œuvre est l'image, mais dehors il y a ce qui n'est pas représenté par l'image,
ce qui n'est pas l'image – le désarroi, l'exécution, c'est-à-dire le réel, le seul
et strict réel qui ne doit rien ni à l'histoire ni à la prise de vue. Qui n'est ni
à voir, ni à dire.*

Given that the currency is counterfeit,
the meaning of the image changes irre-
vocably. False money. Act of war.
It all depends on which end of the lens
is used: question of focus, question of
angle also. Not viburnum or scabious,
a bit of devilry's necessary (essential)
or else (if not) the legend will vanish.
(Recording of a disarray then execution
which is not of a political prisoner.)

Currency *and* legend: *a thing said that must be said, not to be signified but to give tone, movement, direction. Currency and legend are recorded: inscribed with a blazon or an illustration. This whole poem is written beneath or beside the photograph of Sámano who is about to be executed. An inscription which is not in the work. The work is the image, but what is not represented by the image lies outside it, that which is not the image – the disarray, the execution, which is to say the real, the only and literal real which owes nothing to either the story or the camera shot. Which cannot be seen or said.*

Dans le conte d'Andersen, les flocons de neige pareils à des abeilles blanches ont une reine, grande, belle et froide. Avant de retourner dans son royaume, La Reine des Neiges passe dans une des rues du conte et à l'instant les fenêtres se couvrent de fleurs de gel. Munie d'un traîneau à propulseur intégré de flocons neigeux et d'un grand manteau verglacé, La Reine des Neiges ne constitue pas vraiment un modèle de réchauffement (aussi, se blottir dans ses bras est un pari risqué contre la mort, sous peine de glaciation immédiate) et son régiment de flocons la protège en rangs serrés (hérissons blancs, ours rebondis, paquets de serpents : une armée de neige vivante, en somme). Son château constitué de poussières de neige n'a ni portes ni fenêtres. Au centre de cette forteresse aussi légère et volatile que la paille, un lac glacé faisant office de trône.

La légende devient le conte, et le conte est le conte du gel. C'est clair, c'est un pari contre la mort. Pari perdu, pari gagné en le perdant : la légende gèle avec la Reine qu'elle étreint. Les mots « lac glacé » se font entendre comme assonance en stalactite des mots « langue », « lexique » ou « glossaire » – et « glose » n'est pas loin, qui n'est rien d'autre que cela que j'essaie de produire ici. Légende gelée : voilà l'œuvre du silencing*. On ne s'occupe pas de l'histoire de Sámano, de sa mort héroïque ou de son insolence téméraire, on s'occupe de cela par quoi cette mort gèle en nous la parole, stoppe les mots, gerce les lèvres et nous débarrasse de tous les contes de la littérature accommodante et spectaculaire. L'eau de rose gèle, et la pensée réfléchie fait de même.*

Les contes sont pour les enfants. Les enfants sont ceux qui ne parlent pas. Les contes ne sont pas faits pour être crus, mais pour être mangés crus, comme la langue.

In the Andersen fairytale, snowflakes
hover like white bees around their
queen, tall, beautiful and cold. Before
returning to her realm, The Snow Queen
walks down one of the streets in the tale
and every window blooms with flowers
of frost. Riding a sled with internal
snowflake propulsion, swathed in a large,
black-iced cape, The Snow Queen's
never considered a model of warmth
(snuggling in her arms is a risky bet
with death, on pain of being frozen
in a flash). Her frosty regiments protect
her in tight ranks (white hedgehogs,
rotund bears, packs of snakes: in short,
an army of living snow). Her castle is
built of powdery snow with no doors no
windows. In the center of this fortress
as light and airy as chaff, a frozen lake
serves as her throne.

The legend becomes a fairytale, and the fairytale is the story of ice.
It is clear, it is a bet with death. A bet lost, a bet won in the losing: the legend
freezes with the Queen it holds tight. We hear in the assonance of the words
"frozen" and "throne" a stalactite of words like "tongue," "lexicon" or "glossary"
– not far from "gloss," which is nothing more than what I am trying to do here.
Frozen legend: here is the work of silencing. We do not care about the story
of Sámano, about his heroic death or his reckless insolence, we care about how
this death freezes speech inside us, stops our words, chaps our lips, rids us of the
literature of comfortable, fabulous stories. Rose water freezes, and reflective
thought does, too.
    Fairytales are for children. Children are the ones who do not speak.
Fairytales are not made to hold true, but to be swallowed whole, like language.

En fumant / les derniers instants / de mon
cigare / en les confrontant / dans le même tissu
de toile / avec des images à coupe automatique /
c'est-à-dire sans signification delibérée / mais
froidement glaciales / / j'avance mon armée /
(Tous sont flocons de neige vivants) / (un éclat
dans l'œil et voilà le cœur piqué / le cœur pareil
à un bloc de glace / j'avance / en belligérante
vitalité / c'est à moi / de donner / le signal / de
leur exécution /

*Coupe automatique : il faut que ça coupe et que ça se coupe tout seul,
de soi, sans autre dessein ni mécanisme que ce déclenchement automobile et
autotélique de la coupe.*

La coupe – la barre de fraction, l'enjambement, le versus *raide du*
prorsus *(cela d'où vient la « prose », l'aller-tout-droit-devant), la bascule
et le versant du bout de ligne, la ligne alignée non pas sur la page ou la
marge mais sur une propre contrainte intérieure et autochtone qui s'exécute
impeccablement froidement par une lame immanente à la langue : voilà, la
coupe est pleine, c'est ainsi que le poème verse par-dessus bord sa plus propre
substance et son cœur véritable.*

By smoking / the last moments / of my
cigar / facing them / in the same canvas
clip / with images cut automatically /
which is to say with no deliberate meaning /
with glacial cold / / my army advances /
(All of it living snowflakes) / a splinter
in the eye and heart's pierced / the heart
is a block of ice / I advance / bellicosely
vibrant / It's me / who gives / the order /
they execute /

*Automatic cut: that it must cut and that it cuts all alone, by itself,
without any device or mechanism other than this automobilic, autotelic
activation of the cut.*

The cut – bar of fraction, stroke of enjambment, the rigid versus
of prorsus *(where prose comes from, that going-straight-ahead), the swing
and turn at the end of the line, the line aligning not with the page or margin
but with its own internal and autochthonous constraint, impeccably, coldly
executed by the sword of immanence in language. Here's the cut running over:
the poem filling to the brim and pouring its heart out.*

Neutralité : vous m'avez demandé d'être neutre,
pas étonnant que je neutralise tout, après.

Après / une certaine quantité / de mouvement /
nulle / pour ainsi dire / se déplace / avec moi / le
curseur / sans la légende / je suis dépossédée / se
déplace / et l'image / ne m'appartient plus / elle
est / pour ainsi dire / *como nullo* / pour ainsi dire /
un mouvement partagé / sans effet observable /
que je transporte avec moi /

Elle met le curseur sur le bout de sa langue.

Se neutralise peu à peu ma bouche,
Avec la sienne désemparée.

Il faut que le débord du poème suive très exactement les bords de
la langue, et passe de l'un à l'autre, locuteur à lecteur, sans intervalle. Mais
ce qu'il suit ainsi, c'est la dépossession elle-même, dont les bords partout
coïncident avec les lèvres de la langue. Les lèvres de la plaie langagière.
Pourquoi des poètes ? Inutile d'ajouter en temps ou en tant de
détresse. Cela va de soi : le pourquoi des poètes est la plainte (non pas la
question) de la détresse même. Ils nous disent pourquoi et pour quoi, par
quelle raison et à quelle fin la langue se neutralise et se résorbe et se dérobe
et se déborde. La langue échappe à son office, à savoir de faire paraître les
choses en tant que choses et le monde en tant que monde, et nous souffrons
que cela ne paraisse point.
Mais les poètes nous disent aussi qu'il en va de la sorte parce qu'il
n'y a pas d'en tant que, ni des choses, ni du monde. C'est là que la langue
blesse : la chose en tant que chose devient aussitôt autre chose.

Neutrality: you asked me to be neutral,
no surprise, after that, I neutralize everything.

After / a certain amount / of movement /
nothing / one might say / is displaced / with
me / the cursor / without the legend / I'm
dispossessed / displaced / the image / no longer
mine / it is / one might say / *como nullo* /
one might say / a movement shared / to no
observable effect / is what I bring with me

She puts the cursor on the tip of her tongue.

Neutralizing my mouth little by little,
With hers helpless.

    The overflow of the poem must follow very exactly the borders of
language, passing from one to the other, speaker to reader, with no interval.
But what follows is dispossession itself, whose borders coincide with the lip of
language. The lip of the linguistic wound.
    Why are there poets? Useless to add at such times of so much
anguish. It goes without saying: the why of poets is to lament (not to question)
anguish itself. They tell us why and what for, for what reason and to what
end language neutralizes itself and is absorbed, slipping away, overflowing.
Language evades its office, namely to make things seem so much like things
and the world so much like a world, and we suffer when they do not seem like
themselves.
    But poets also tell us that it gets this way because there is no such thing
as so much like, not for things, not for the world. That is where language wounds
us: the thing so much like a thing has instantly become something else.

Un mouvement partagé par plusieurs corps
n'influe pas /
Prenez 1 dictateur + 1 dictateur / ça nous fait
2 dictateurs /
Ça nous fait un sous-titre et demi qui n'influe
pas /

Le dictateur est aussi, nécessairement, le poème qui dicte impérieusement sa langue et sa cadence, sa coupe et son débord, son influx, son reflux. Sa dictature me coupe le discours. L'indigence et l'excès de cet empire sont la même chose, une même pauvreté orgueilleuse.

A movement which several bodies share
impacts nothing /
Take 1 dictator + 1 dictator / that makes
2 dictators /
One and a half subheadings which impact
nothing /

The dictator is also, necessarily, the poem, which imperiously dictates its language and cadence, its cut and its overflow, its flux and influx. The poem's dictatorship cuts short my discourse. The indigence and excess of its empire are one and the same, the same fierce poverty.

Effet massicot de l'image.

Écho du mot massé, instantané photo.

The guillotined effect of the image.

Echo of the sheared word, the snapshot.

J'affronte et je fuis. Tranchant de l'image : je vois du sang, me coupe, panse la plaie, sans perdre connaissance cette fois je le lèche bien en face droit dans les yeux injectés de Fortino, j'affronte je soutiens son regard, c'est un printemps Marnie loin-sous-les-bombes, un printemps digne de l'été et en cela presque obscène avec ses robes et ses jupes flambant neuf, ses mules, ses forsythias jaune d'or, ses dj volatiles. C'est un printemps qui perd son sang après un régime idéologique drastique et tu me demandes, tu insistes – comment ça va ?

Merci, ça ira. Pourquoi me demandes-tu ça ? Tu sais que ton tranchant me coupe. Tu sais que je soutiens mal ton regard. Que la dispute est très ancienne entre philosophie et poésie : Platon déjà disait cela. Tu sais que ton printemps et ton allure flambante, la polyglottie de tes noms Fortino Virginie Marnie, tu sais que cela m'étourdit comme pas une idée, pas un concept n'en est capable. Tu sais que tu me fais perdre mon sang – et ainsi te répondre. Ça va dans cette hémorragie de sens que tu as provoquée.

Je m'entends malgré moi te répondre « ça va ». Car le sans-fond résonne et ne fait que ça : c'est pourquoi jamais un poète ne confond la détresse avec le nihilisme.

I face it and flee. The image's sharp edge:
I see the blood, cut myself, dress the gash,
not losing consciousness this time I lick it
in front of the bloodshot eyes of Fortino,
I look him right in the eye, it's spring,
a Marnie remote-from-the-bombs spring
ready for summer, almost obscene with its
dresses and spanking new skirts, its mules,
its yellow-gold forsythias, ephemeral dj.
It's a spring that has lost so much blood
after an ideological drastic regime and
you ask me, you insist – how's it going?

*Fine, thank you. Why do you ask? You know that your sharp edge
cuts me. You know that I cannot bear your gaze. That the argument between
philosophy and poetry is very old: Plato already said all this. You know that
your spring and blazing style – the polyglot of your names Fortino Virginie
Marnie – you know this stuns me as not even ideas, not even concepts can. You
know that you make me sweat blood – and so I answer you back. But it goes
with the hemorrhage of meaning that you have provoked.*

*I hear myself answer in spite of myself, "Fine." For the abysmal
resounds and that is the only thing it does: this is why a poet never confuses
anguish with nihilism.*

– Je sais me mettre en rang
– Je n'oublie pas mon service
– Je lève le doigt pour parler
– Je ne pose pas de questions idiotes
– Je fais rarement des fautes de copie
– (J'ai toujours mon matériel sur moi)

(silence, césure)

- I know how to get in line
- I never forget my duty
- I raise my hand to speak
- I never ask dumb questions
- I rarely make typos
- (I always bring what I need)

(silence, caesura)

D'où vient qu'il est absolument en mouvement et
absolument immobile en même temps ?
Est-ce parce qu'éloigné de son lieu, il cherche
absolument à y retourner ? Ou bien qu'il l'occupe
absolument ?
Un corps en mouvement laisse parfois des traces
dans les corps immobiles. D'où l'effet neigeux de
l'image : chaque chose à sa place est absolument
en mouvement est absolument au repos.

(silence encore, chute de neige)

How can he be absolutely in motion and
absolutely motionless at the same time?
Is it because, far from his place, he seeks
absolutely to return there? Or to occupy it
absolutely?
A body in motion sometimes leaves traces
in motionless bodies. From which the snowy
image: each thing in its place is absolutely in
motion is absolutely at rest.

(still silence, snowfall)

Un amour possiblement un amour pour les
baies de viorne et les scabieuses, ce bouquet

est absolument en mouvement

Fortino l'homme immobile devant le mur d'exécution est immobile-en-mouvement parce qu'il rejoint son lieu, le lieu de sa proximité naturelle et familière, la mort, le sang séché, la fumée dissipée. Il rejoint ce lieu lointain. La neige qui tombe sur l'image et de l'image immobilise dans l'image ce mouvement d'approche, ce pas au-delà, ce glissement et cette chute au loin. Ainsi se trouve-t-il transformé en bouquet, selon l'analogie de l'être. Fleurs coupées, tranchées, qui doucement absolument laissent remuer leurs noms, lesquels sont des images, c'est-à-dire des lointains surgissant au milieu des mots. La fleur de scabieuse est « d'un bleu mourant » écrit Bernardin de Saint-Pierre. « On la croirait en deuil. On l'appelle aussi, pour cette raison, fleur de veuve. »

Roger Martin du Gard a parlé d'écritures « annelées comme les vrilles de la viorne ». Virginie n'en sait peut-être rien, mais elle n'en a pas besoin pour être véritablement elle-même, en personne, l'écriture veuve de Fortino, et ces fleurs fragiles près de son corps exécuté.

A love possibly a love for the berries of
virburnum and scabious, this bouquet

is absolutely in motion

*Fortino the motionless man in front of the wall of execution is
unmoving-in-motion because he returns to his place, the place of his natural
and familiar proximity, death, dried blood, dispelled smoke. He returns to
this faraway place. The snow that falls on the image and from the image stills
this movement of approach in the image, this step beyond, this slipping and
falling in the distance. So he is transformed into a bouquet of flowers, in the
analogy to being. Cut flowers, cuttings, which gently, absolutely allow their
names to shift, which are images, one might say faraways springing up among
the words. The flower of the scabiosa, writes Bernardin de Saint-Pierre, is "a
deathly blue": "One might imagine that it is in mourning. For this reason, it is
called the widow's flower."*

*Roger Martin du Gard speaks of script "ringed like the shoots of
viburnum." Virginie may not know all that, but she does not need to, to be
genuinely herself, in person, the widow-writing of Fortino, and these fragile
flowers near his executed body.*

Blanc, elle a voulu un blanc.
Entre strophe et strophe. Marquer le temps, le
vide du temps, le passage.

White, she wanted a whiteness.
Between strophe and strophe. To mark time, the emptiness
of time, its passing.

Hélices ou boucles flèches. Faible distance.
En baladant une épaisseur par exemple – nous
échappe – nous proposons d'entrer en résis-
tance. Une résistance de l'ordre de la taille
d'un cheveu après une division par 100 000.

*Résistance de la poésie : résistance de rien, d'un infiniment petit. De
ce qui ne finit pas les mots, ne finit pas le sens, fuit et nous fait fuir avec. Cette
épaisseur sans épaisseur fait pièce au discours, se dérobe, se défile. Mais ce n'est
pas comme une extase apocalyptique et suressentielle. C'est la pensée d'une
échappée de pensée.*

Helixes or loops arrows. Short distance.
In toting around a thickness for example –
escapes us – we suggest joining in resis-
tance. A resistance on the order of a hair's
breadth after being divided by 100,000.

Poetry's resistance: resistance of nothing, of an infinitesimal. Of that
which does not finish words, does not finish meaning, flees and makes us flee
with it. This thickness without thickness stymies speech, shies away from, slips
off. But it is not like an apocalyptic and supraëssential ecstasy. It is the thought
of the escape of thought.

En une nanoseconde
une nanorésistance
nanoréfie l'espace-temps

L'infiniment petit passe encore entre poésie et philosophie. Il passe infiniment mince, dérivée interminable à la tangence de leurs deux hélices (comme formant une autre hélice de l'ADN de Crick et Watson, un autre vrille d'un autre code génétique, celui de la bête à parole, du zôon logon ekôn, l'« animal doué de langage » ou l'« animal ayant langage » – mais que veulent dire « être doué de » et « avoir » ? Ne serait-ce pas plutôt lui qui nous « a », lui le langage ?). Le poème dit : vous vous faites avoir !

De là que Platon soutienne qu'il nous ment.

Le philosophe dit qu'on ne l'aura pas. En effet, on n'a rien de lui, sinon ce qui peut en rester et qui, lorsque cela arrive, n'est pas autre chose qu'un peu de poésie.

.

In a nanosecond
a nanoresistance
nanoreifies space-time

    The infinitesimal still comes between poetry and philosophy. It slips by infinitely slightly, stemming endlessly from the tangent of their two helixes (as if forming another DNA helix to the double helix of Crick and Watson, another shoot of another genetic code, that of the beast with speech, of the zôon logon ekôn, *the "animal endowed with language" or the "animal having language" – but what is the meaning of "to be endowed with" and "to have"? Doesn't it "have" us instead, it being language?). The poem says: you've been had!*

    From there Plato could claim that it was lying to us.

    The philosopher says that he won't be had. In effect, we get nothing from him except that which can be left, and which, when it occurs, is nothing other than a bit of poetry.

me font simultanément l'effet d'un champs de
renoncules qui s'invite chez moi et que je
plastifie, faute d'y croire.

*Une simultanéité fait la question récurrente de son poème. Celle de
la vie et de la mort de Fortino Sámano face aux fusils, celle de son cigare, de
son sourire et de son sang, celle de l'image et de l'absence à jamais, celle de
l'infiniment petit et d'un lac tout entier gelé, celle du regard sur l'image et
de l'image qui scrute le regard. Et celle d'une description pensive et d'une
pensée acérée. « Renoncule » est un terme précis (« petite grenouille » : c'est
la renoncule aquatique) autant qu'évasif, enroulé dans son premier segment,
clair et distinct dans le second. Telle est sa valeur plastique, celle que chaque
mot attend lorsqu'il s'invite chez nous hors de son usage. Le simultané du
signifié et du plastifié, le gel luisant du cours du sens, voilà le rendez- vous.*

*. . . sauf qu'il était raté : Virginie me l'avoue, une fois qu'elle m'a lu, elle voulait
écrire «que je plastique » ; les renoncules devaient exploser, comme la grenouille de
la fable sans doute ; mais nous décidons de garder son lapsus ; comme s'il n'y en avait
pas à chaque pas, comme si poésie n'était pas lapsus continu, un mot pour un autre et
laisser passer la pulsion ; enfin, l'explosion fige aussi, gélifie un état des lieux.*

giving me simultaneously the impression of
a buttercup field inviting itself home with me
which I plastic-coat instead of believe in.

*Simultaneity brings us to the recurring question in her poem.
That of the life and death of Fortino Sámano in front of the guns, that of
his cigar, of his smile and of his blood, of the image and of eternal absence, of
the infinitesimal and of a frozen lake, of the gaze regarding the image and
of the image scrutinizing the gaze. And that of a pensive description and of
a pointed thought. "Buttercup" is a precise term ("little frog": is the aquatic
buttercup) but also evasive, wound into the first segment, clear and distinct in
the second. Such is its plastic value, in which each word waits until we invite it
in out of usage. The simultaneity of the signified and of the plastic-coated, the
gleaming gel of meaning's course, here's the encounter . . .*

*. . . except that it failed: Virginie admits to me, once she read this, that she had meant
to write "plastic-explosives"; the buttercups were to explode, no doubt like the frog in
Fontaine's fable; but we have decided to retain her slip; as if there aren't slips at every
step, as if poetry weren't a continual slippage, one word for another and let the urge
pass; at last, the explosion congeals, too, gelling the scene.*

D'où vient qu'en le voyant nous ayons l'intui-
tion directe de la simultanéité ? D'où vient
que je suis là – je suis sous les bombes aient lieu
au même instant sur deux théâtres distincts ?
D'où vient cette voix, qui semble demander
« tout va bien » ?

*D'où vient ? D'un endroit irrécupérable. L'original, le négatif de
l'image de Sámano, et même pas, si d'une photo l'original n'est que dehors, au
temps et lieu d'une pression d'une nanoseconde du doigt sur le déclencheur de
l'appareil. L'original d'une photo est ce déclic de capture et de fuite simultanées.
L'image plie les deux en soi. Il en sort cette voix qui nous demande si tout va
bien. Tout ? Il s'agit en effet chaque fois de tout, de la totalité du dicible et
de l'indicible, tout entière déclarée parfaitement une et impeccablement divisée
entre la voix qu'on entend et son émission improbable et inaudible.*

*Nul n'est quitte de cette question : d'où vient l'instant présent et sa
partition en deux et plus de deux ? Notez-le, Virginie parle ici philosophie :
« l'intuition directe de la simultanéité ». Elle capte insidieusement ma langue,
elle la détourne – et que s'est-il donc passé ? Les concepts sont devenus des
intuitions, le concept d'« intuition » tout le premier. Ce n'est pas que je ne les
entende plus en tant que concepts d'entendement, c'est que les mots en même
temps – simultanément – font glisser sur ma langue leurs corps, leurs saveurs,
leurs lueurs. « Intuition » est le mot glissant qui provoque ici ce glissement que
« directe » poursuit en brusquant la cadence et en frappant une battue sonore
entre les chuintements et les sinuosités des deux mots qui l'entourent.*

*Mais par là le débord théorique du poème me conduit à cette pensée,
que ces bruissements du concept ne sont pas moins audibles dans le texte de
la philosophie, malgré tous les efforts que fait ce texte pour les résoudre en
composition d'idéalités.*

When we see him, why do we feel the direct intuition of simultaneity? Why when I'm here – am I under bombs falling at the same time on two separate stages? Why this voice that seems to be asking, "everything all right"?

Where does it come from? From an irretrievable place. The original, the negative of Sámano's image, or not even that, whether of any photograph, the original is only the outside, in the time and place of the nanosecond in which the finger clicked the camera's shutter release. The original of a photograph is this click of simultaneous capture and flight. The image folds both into itself. This voice comes from it asking us if everything is all right. Everything? Each time, it is about everything, in effect, about the totality of the sayable and the unsayable, declared altogether perfectly whole and impeccably divided between the voice one hears and its improbable, inaudible utterance.

No one is quit of the question: where does this moment in the present and its splitting into two or more than two come from? Notice here that Virginie is speaking philosophy: "direct intuition of simultaneity." She catches my language insidiously, she twists it – then what has happened? The concepts have become intuitions, the concept of "intuition" first and foremost. It's not that I don't understand them any longer as concepts of understanding, but that words – simultaneously – make their letters, their flavors, their glimmers slip over my tongue. "Intuition" is the slippery word here that provokes such slipping, which "direct" anticipates in sharpening the cadence and striking a brisk beat before the sibilant hiss and sinuosity of the words that follow.

And so the poem's overflow of theory leads me to think that these murmurs of concepts aren't less audible in the philosophical text, despite all the efforts this text makes to resolve them into a composition of idealities.

Si, descendant de la rame du métro, l'aveugle
me dit « Attention, vous avez une marche », il
n'y aura pas la moindre once de condescend-
dance ni d'amertume dans sa voix. Juste une
certaine solidarité certaine. L'image ne dit
rien d'autre que cela : « Attention, vous avez
une marche » et je la rate, comme de bien
entendu, m'affale puis rebondis sur le sol ;
blessée, non, légèrement – c'est-à-dire à vie –
j'écris une lance dans chaque jambe : une
plaque s'est détachée.

Les idéalités ne sont pas simplement opposées aux valeurs, c'est-à-dire
aux tonalités, aux résonances, assonances, présences et distances que l'image
dispose. Les idéalités ne sont pas sans nuances ni vibrations. Elles ne sont
pas sans intonations. L'idée aveugle – Homère, l'idéal du poème – avertit de
ceci, que le sol est écarté d'elle par une marche. La poète s'affale, comme une
voile sur le pont. Le poète de Baudelaire perdait son auréole dans le ruisseau.
Celle-ci se blesse et se répare de prothèses chirurgicales. L'aura est la double
cicatrice. Pourquoi de toujours le poète est-il blessé ? Légèrement, sans doute,
ici, mais blessé malgré tout. Blessé et cicatrisé d'une chute primitive. Dans
le péché originel, le philosophe est mal : il le récuse ou bien s'affole de ce qu'il
macule la raison même. Dans ce péché, le poète a mal. C'est la langue qui
défaille, le langage qui faute, « comme de bien entendu » dit-elle à la façon
de la chanson. La faute et sa blessure, sa cicatrice, c'est l'aura, ce n'est rien
d'autre que la lumière de la chute elle-même. Comment ces mots seuls, « une
plaque se détache », détachés eux-mêmes d'un corps ici dissimulé, abstraits
d'une tectonique gardée secrète, comment ces mots touchent l'oreille, je veux
dire l'âme, comment leur blessure résonne dans un écho mat.

If, as I exit a subway car, the blind man
calls to me, "Watch out! There's a step,"
he won't have one ounce of condescension
or bitterness in his voice. Just a certain
assertion of solidarity. The image says
nothing besides this: "Watch out! There's
a step" but I miss it, naturally, and fall
down then jump back up on the platform;
hurt, no, slightly – what I mean is for life –
I write with a lance in each leg: a patch
scraped off.

Idealities are not merely opposed to values, that is, to tonality, resonance, assonance, to the presence and distance that the image posits. Idealities are not without nuances and vibrations. They have various intonations. The blind idea – Homer, poetry's ideal – warns about this, that the ground is farther than one thought because there is a step. The poet falls over, like a sail onto a deck. Baudelaire's poet lost his halo in a gutter. This one hurts and mends herself with surgical prostheses. The aura is a double scar. Why are poets always hurt? Here, no doubt slightly, but hurt nonetheless. Hurt and scarring over from a primordial fall. The philosopher is not comfortable with original sin: either he refutes it or falls dumb because it stains reason itself. But the poet is wounded by this sin. It is language that falters, language at fault, "naturally," as she says like an old refrain. The sin and the wound, the scar, which is the aura, which is nothing other than the light from the fall itself. How mere words, "a patch scraped off," themselves are scraped off from a body concealed here, abstracted from a tectonic kept in secret, how these words touch the ear, I want to say the soul, how their wound reverberates in dull echo.

Lunette d'approche / je vois le peloton d'exé-
cution / mais je ne vois pas mon ombre / Es
ist die Rede (*erste Erinnerung*) / c'est l'histoire /
j'ai perdu mon image / Que nul ne boive plus
cette eau ou en pierre se changera

Retour sur image. Celle-ci est retournée, c'est le peloton et Virginie est au lieu de Fortino, mêlée à lui. De là elle voit qu'elle n'a plus son image. Retour au domaine des contes. La femme sans ombre et l'homme qui a perdu la sienne. Ce qui est sans ombre, la lumière le traverse entièrement. Désirer laisser passer la lumière, s'effacer devant elle, disparaître en elle : Goethe au moment de son exécution, « mehr Licht ». Retour à l'allemand, souvenir (Erinnerung, c'est-à-dire intériorisation, absorption, incorporation). Mais Virginie ne traduit pas, comme de bien entendu car comment faire entendre die Rede *: la parole, le discours, le propos, le langage en acte, en discours, en flux, loquace, élocutoire. Comment ? Le poème est la pierre en laquelle est changée l'eau inaudible de la* Rede.

Telescopic lens / I can see the firing
squad / but not my shadow / Es ist die
Rede (*erste Erinnerung*) / In this story /
I lost my image / Let no one drink the
water lest he be turned to stone

Freeze frame on image. This one is reversed, it is the firing squad
and Virginie is in the place where Fortino is, blended with him. From
there she sees that she no longer has his image before her. Freeze frame on
fairytales. The woman without a shadow and the man who lost his. That
which has no shadow, light goes entirely through it. To wish to let light
pass through, to efface oneself before it, to disappear into it: Goethe at the
moment of his death, "mehr Licht." Freeze frame on German, on memories
(Erinnerung, that is, internalization, absorption, incorporation). But
Virginie does not translate, naturally, for how else to make die Rede *heard:*
speech, discourse, words, language in action, in speech, in flux, loquacious,
elocuted. How? The poem is the stone into which the inaudible waters of
the Rede *have been changed.*

Faites encore une fois l'essai de votre ombre /

D'un fil je me découvre / mais c'est vous qui dis-
paraissez /
Tué / je vous tue / seul tutoiement possible / mon
effigie reste / quand rien de vous n'est visible /

*Haletant, à nouveau fractionné, souffle coupé, ému il tutoie : tu est
un appel à l'absolu de l'autre, à l'absolu en lui, à sa mort increvable, ou bien à
Dieu, comme en anglais, ou bien, autre version, à l'amour ou à l'amitié. Tu,
sans doute, dit toujours « tu me tues ». Tu m'exécutes, tu me mets à bout de
dire et de faire signe.*

Try one more time with your shadow /

I pick off one thread / but it's you who dis-
appear /
Killed / I kill you / can only call you close /
my effigy remains / but nothing of you does /

Gasping, fragmented anew, breathless, moved, he calls you *close:*
you *is an intimate appeal to the absolute of the other, to the absolute in himself,*
to his indestructible death, or to God, as they say in English, or in another
version, to love and to friendship. You *no doubt always says "you're killing*
me." You execute me, push me to the limits to say and to give a sign.

Trois tours de muscle. Je suis en prison. Rien
à se mettre sous la dent à la bibliothèque
carcérale. J'y vais pourtant de mes sugges-
ions d'achat. Bibliothèque vide, j'obtiens
cependant l'adresse d'un éditeur, puis deux,
puis trois. J'écris aux auteurs. « Qu'avez-vous
fait ? » me demande-t-on. Je suis tous cou-
pables et doublement puni : ne pouvant lire,
je ne lis plus : donc, j'écris puis me lis. Tous
coupables.

*Fortino Sámano, devant mourir, se souvient de la prison. C'est là
qu'il s'est fait écrivain : pour pouvoir lire. Lire, c'est la faute : c'est vouloir être
comme des dieux qui jouent avec le chiffre des choses. Et si j'écris moi-même
ce chiffre, c'est infâme, je confisque le monde. L'infamie toujours imminente
de la poésie se tient dans cette confiscation. La philosophie, qui paraît vouloir
dominer, cède toujours devant le monde, rajoute un labeur de plus et diffère
encore le chiffre.*

Mais la poésie . . . J'entends ce crissement de vieille plume : donc
j'écris puis me lis. *Cela grince mais il faut en passer par là, ne pas sauter par-
dessus les mots, et par conséquent tenir bon sur la crête risquée du chiffre. Si
la poésie ne renonce pas à déchiffrer, et à refaire à neuf chaque fois son propre
chiffre, c'est qu'elle en passe par les mots, que la philosophie toujours espère
dissiper, voire éviter complètement.*

*Prenez ici « Trois tours de muscle ». Ça vous a tout de suite serré
dans une constriction. Le mot « muscle » est musclé, en effet, et vous ne vous
débarrassez pas facilement, vieux philosophe, de cette très vieille créance que
vous vouliez retirer à Cratyle. Tours de muscle, prison, tours d'écrou, tours en
rond dans la cellule, gymnastique solitaire pour se maintenir, aller-retour à la
bibliothèque vide, muscles des mains crispées sur le crayon crissant.*

Three turns for the muscles. I'm in jail.
Nothing in the prison library to sink my
teeth into. I go there with my helpful
suggestions of books to buy. Library
empty, I find a publisher's address, then
a second, and a third. I write the authors.
"What did you do?" I'm asked. All guilty,
I'm doubly punished: forbidden to read,
I can't read: so I write then read myself.
All guilty.

Fortino Sámano, before dying, remembers the prison. It is there he became a writer himself: to be able to read. To read is the crime: it is to want to be like gods playing with the cipher of things. And to write this cipher myself is shameful; I'm confiscating the world. Poetry's ever-impending shame lies in this confiscation. Philosophy, though it seems to want to dominate, always yields to the world, adds another labor, and defers the cipher again.

But poetry . . . I hear the scratching of an old quill: so I write then read myself. *This is grating but there is no way around it, not to skip over the words, and consequently, to stand firm upon the cipher's dangerous crest. If poetry refuses to abandon deciphering, making its own cipher new each time, it is because it goes by words, which philosophy always hopes to clear away, indeed to avoid completely.*

Take, for example, "Three turns for the muscles." *Right away a constriction's binding you. The word "muscle" is muscled, in effect, and you cannot easily rid yourself, old philosopher, of this ancient credit you wanted to redeem from Cratylus. Turns for the muscles, prison, turn of the screw, turns around the cell, solitary gymnastics to stay fit, back and forth in the empty library, the muscles of the hand clenching the pen scratching away.*

avril je ne savais pas, mai j'appris, juin je notais

Pour noter ça, nous faire lire ça, il faut une décision, un aplomb que je n'aurais pas.

Chronologie calendaire du « je ». Cogito mensualisé et cumulant son propre processus dans une assonance mouillée – « juin je » – précédée du mouvement dialectique – « ne savais pas mais j'appris ». Enfin, je noté, chiffré et du même coup déchiffré par lui-même.

(Mais aussi, à propos d'avril, rappelez-vous, elle avait dit auparavant « D'un fil je me découvre ». Elle transgresse le proverbe en montrant un peu de sa peau ; ce pourrait être une définition très provisoire de la poésie : parole nue non proverbiale.)

April I did not know, May I was learning, June I took note

In order to note that, to make us read that, one needs a decisiveness, a self-possession that I would not have.

Chronological calendar of the "I." A monthly cogito that records its own process with soft assonance –"June I took note" – preceded by a dialectical movement – "I did not know may I be learning." Finally, "I" noted, enciphering and in the same stroke deciphering by itself.

(But also, apropos of May, remember she had said before, "I pick off one thread." She ignores the proverb by showing a bit of skin; it could be a very provisional definition of poetry: non-proverbial naked speech.)

Les mots qui te reviennent les revenants avec les injures les premières phrases formées forment une langue ta langue *unelangue* revenant elle revient aux mots

La langue fait retour, c'est-à-dire qu'elle puise dans une immémorialité absolue, dans un passé à jamais dépassé dont elle reprend pourtant l'ouverture et le passage. Les premières phrases, l'invention du lié, du tenu, du tendu de mot à mot, la modulation mienne de ce qu'on nomme le phrasé, mon style, mon ton, l'inimitable, l'unique absolument de mon intonation, de mon inclination. Ce que recherche en vain avec ferveur l'agitation des théoriciens du « genre » : si j'ai parlé en genre élevé, moyen ou bas, en diégèse pure ou bien en mimèse pure ou mixte, en épique, tragique ou comique ou lyrique ou didactique . . . Comment, oui, comment tu parles, toi ?

Mais la langue revient aux mots : voilà qui est plus sévère et plus difficile. Les mots seuls, déliés en parataxe, proférés en injures, c'est-à-dire en faiseurs de tort. Le mot fait tort à la chose et tort à mon désir de dire. Mais il revient, il hante en revenant mes journées et mes silences. Il m'inquiète.

Words come back to you like ghosts with their insults the first formed
sentences forming a language your language *onelanguage* which
returning returns you to words

*Language comes back, drawn from an absolute immemoriality,
from a past forever bygone, to which it nevertheless, passing through the
opening, returns. The first sentences, the invention of binding, of holding,
of setting word next to word, the modulation mine, that which one calls
phrasing, my style, my tone, the inimitable, the absolute uniqueness of my
intonation, of my inclination. What the theorists of "genre" have sought
in vain with restless fervor: whether I have been speaking in a genre high,
middle, or low, in pure diegesis or in pure or mixed mimesis, in epic, tragic,
comic, lyric or didactic . . . How, yes, how are you yourself speaking?*

*But language comes back to the words: this is both more severe and
more difficult. Words alone, released into parataxis, uttered as insults, that is,
causing harm. The word harms the thing and harms my desire to speak. But
it comes back, it haunts my days and silences. It troubles me.*

Je ne sais pas comment faire. Comment tu fais,
toi ? Comment la poser ma langue, dis ? Ma
langue aphasique ? Comment ?
Je parle et je n'ai plus d'image mentale du mot ; je
lis et il me faudrait des images, un livre illustré
pour chaque mot ; j'écris, ma tête est comme un
puzzle et je ne sais plus ranger : pour « huit » JE
dit « rouge », pour « cinq » JE dit « vert ».
Comment je fais ? Eh bien, c'est simple, je scanne
ce sentiment puis je le retravaille jusqu'à ce que
toute trace disparaisse.

J'ai cru, moi, qu'elle m'interrogeait sur ma façon de faire. Mais c'est
elle-même qui a répondu à ma place. Bien sûr, nul ne peut poser – comme elle
dit – la langue d'un autre. Encore moins si c'est une autre, peut-être, une autre
que moi masculin. Est-ce que cela compte ici ? Allez savoir.
« . . .jusqu'à ce que toute trace disparaisse » : ce qui reste indécis,
c'est de quoi la trace disparaît. Est-ce du mot, ou bien du sentiment ? Il n'est
pas vraisemblable que ce soit du second, puisque c'est lui qu'elle retravaille, en
quoi il est exclu qu'elle l'élimine, à quelque degré qu'elle le transforme. C'est
donc le mot, le chiffre « huit » qui disparaît en rouge dans sa propre vibration
élocutoire. Il s'évapore, il se distille, il se sublime en rouJE.

I don't know how it's done. How do you
do that? How do you put that in language?
My aphasic language? How?
I speak but have no mental images for words
anymore; I read but need pictures from an
illustrated book for each word; I write
but my head is a puzzle and I don't know
how things go anymore: for "eight" **I** say
"red," for "five" **I** say "green."
What can I do? It's really quite simple, I scan
this feeling then work it through until every
trace disappears.

I believed that she was asking me about my way of doing things. But she herself answered in my place. Of course, no one can tell someone else – as she says – how to put it. Still less if that other is a woman, perhaps, someone other than me as male. Does that matter here? Doubt it.

". . .until every trace disappears": what is indefinite is the trace of what is disappearing. Is it of the word, or of the feeling? It is unlikely to be the latter, since she is reworking *it, so we can exclude the possibility that she eliminates it, whatever degree to which she is able to transform it. Then it's the word, the cipher "eight" that disappears into red in its own elocutionary vibration. It evaporates, distills itself, sublimates itself into carmIne red.*

Comment font les gens ? Comment je fais?
J'articule je rééduque je re- du début à la fin
prends le chemin à l'envers de son acquisi-
tion, j'essaie de me souvenir avec mes lèvres,
avec mes joues, avec ma langue puis avec mon
larynx puis avec mon pharynx quand ma tête
ne suit plus ; j'assemble les phonèmes dans
ma bouche si je ne peux plus articuler dans
ma tête <u>silencieusement</u>
<u>Silencieusement</u>, je ne produis rien d'autre
que du silence, aussi mâcher les mots me fait
du bien.

*Les mots ne sont pas faits pour autre chose que pour être mâchés.
Voilà ce qu'il en est du côté de la poésie. « Poème » s'annonce à lui seul déjà
comme un mot mâché avec cette quasi-diphtongue « oè » qui est à elle seule
un nom japonais, prise entre ces deux consonnes si sourdes, p et m où déjà se
meut la mastication. Elle fait remonter les mots de leur mastication jusqu'à
cet inénarrable état de bouillie bredouillée où un jour ils furent acquis, où le
remuement des joues, de la glotte, langue, dents et lèvres soudain se surprit à
mâcher du sens. À cet instant d'une fameuse aphasie apophantique à laquelle
se substitua cette fantastique pharyngie par laquelle il fut désormais inévitable
de ne montrer les choses qu'en montrant aussi les mots comme d'autres choses
mâchées juteuses molles ou coriaces, ligneuses, fibreuses, fondantes, épaisses ou
fluides aux muqueuses.*

How have people done it? How do I?
I enunciate, I rehab, I re- from start to
finish take the route of acquisition in
reverse, try to remember with my lips,
my cheeks, my tongue then with my
larynx then my pharynx when my head
won't follow; I assemble the phonemes
in my mouth if I can no longer enunciate
them in my head silently.
Silently, I produce nothing other than
silence, so chewing words does me
some good.

    Words are not made for anything else than to be chewed. This is what poetry is like: "Poem" makes itself known as a chewed-up word with this quasi-diphthong "oe" – which by itself is a Japanese name – held between these two muffled consonants, p and m, where the chewing is already at work. It brings words up from their mastication to this incredible stew of mumbling mush where they were acquired one day when the movement of cheeks, glottis, tongue, teeth and lips suddenly surprised itself by chewing meaning. At the very instant of a famous apophantic aphasia this pharyngeal fantasy replaced it, after which it was impossible to show only things without also showing words as other chewed things juicy soft or tough, woody, fibrous, melting, thick or flowing mucous.

Je peux longer le mur, je peux compter les
briques, je peux. Je peux me demander combien
de temps ça prendra, je peux me dire que ça
prendra le temps que ça prendra, je peux me dire
que ce temps est bien long mais qu'il est court
aussi. Je peux.

*Mesure de la poésie : la mesure même. Ce dont elle est capable – le peu
qu'elle peut – c'est de compter, et de calculer le compte, d'évaluer le décompte
jusqu'au bout de son exactitude. Poésie charmante et mathématique sévère,
étude de la structure. Théorie du nombre : succession de ses temps, addition
de l'unité à l'unité. Le temps dont elle instaure le comput est pourtant celui de
l'instant de la mort de Fortino.*

*Comptage des briques, mesure du mur : précision, exactitude même
de l'horizon fermé au fond de l'image. Il n'y a rien derrière le mur. Les balles
qui ne seront pas arrêtées dans le corps de Fortino le seront dans le mur. Mais
le mur, lui, ne meurt pas. Le corps de Fortino tombera contre lui, peut-être
glissera contre lui avant de s'affaisser à terre. Tout ira dans le mur, balles et
sang, sourire et fumée, et le poème enfin.*

I can slide along the wall, I can count the
bricks, I can. I can ask myself how much
time this will take, I can tell myself that this
will take the time it takes, I can tell myself
that this time is long enough but it's also
short. I can.

*Poetic measure: the measure itself. What she is able to do – the scant
she can – is to count, and to calculate the count, to estimate the counting right
up to the end of exactness. Charming poetry and severe mathematics, the
study of structure. Theory of numbers: succession of times, the sum of unit over
unit. Yet the time at which she establishes the computation is also the instant
of Fortino's death.*

*Counting the bricks, measuring the wall: precision, exactness even of
the narrow horizon in the image's background. There is nothing behind the
wall. The bullets that Fortino's body could not stop will have been stopped by
the wall. But the wall does not die. Fortino's body will fall against it, perhaps
will slide along it before collapsing on the ground. Everything will go into the
wall, bullets and blood, smile and smoke, and in the end the poem.*

Ici une épithète se détache * cette étoile est
pourtant bien polaire (*her polartime* : un refrain
entêtant s'échappe d'un poème de Dickinson)
et *les vertes prairies font mes noires pensées*
comme si tout adjectif était en soi une épithète
de nature, une redondance et que nous ne
faisions rien d'autre que cela : donner les
définitions des mots que nous plaçons sur la
page, déclinaisons à l'infini.

*La poésie définit : elle assigne à tous les mots leur nature, leur
place, leur inclinaison, déclinaison et entêtement. Ses définitions sont de
véritables finitions. Il ne reste plus rien à attendre ni à tirer des mots. Pas
du moins pour ce poème, pour tel poème qui est son propre espace défini de
définition. Hors de lui, point de salut, tout prendra un autre sens, d'autres
manières de faire et de parler. Ainsi de chaque poème peut sortir un refrain
qui le résume ou qui l'assume. Chacun à son tour se donne son lexique et son
dictionnaire. Chacun se donne sa langue, une langue propre et ainsi le plus
propre de la langue en général. Une langue purement naturelle, entièrement
tirée de son propre fonds lui-même défini à partir de son propre infini et
dans ses limites strictes.*

*La poésie définit. Elle finit. Elle finitise l'infini. Elle lui ouvre
un enclos : l'ensemble des mots, ensemble fini pourtant rendu superposable
ou homogène à la puissance du continu. Infiniment divisible autant que
composable en unités : en atomes déclinant à travers le vide du ciel immense
auquel nous adressons ces prières, ces blasphèmes et euphémismes, ces
imprécations et ces bredouillis qu'un très vieil abus nomme « poèmes ».
Mais une étoile demeure, une polaire inclinaison de notre admiration, de
notre ferveur pour notre page ouverte et tournée vers le ciel.*

Here an epithet comes loose * this star
is in fact polar (*her polartime*: a persistent
refrain escapes from a Dickinson poem)
green meadows make my thoughts black
as if any adjective in itself were an epithet
by nature, a redundancy, so that we do
nothing else besides this: give definitions
for the words we place on the page,
declensions to infinity.

Poetry defines: it assigns all words their nature, their place, their inclination, their declension and obstinacy. Its definitions have a true finish. There is nothing more to expect or pull from words. Not, at least, for this poem, for such a poem creates its own defined sphere of definition. Without that, one's lost, everything will take on another meaning, other ways of acting and speaking. Thus a refrain can emerge from each poem that sums up or assumes it. Each in its turn gives us its lexicon and dictionary. Each gives us its own language, a proper language and thus the most proper to language in general. A purely natural language, drawn wholly from its proper ground, which is defined by its own infinity and within its own strict limits.

Poetry defines. It finishes. It finitizes the infinite, opening up a fold for it: the whole set of words, a finite set nevertheless made superimposable or consistent with the power of the continuum. Infinitely divisible as well as composable into units: into atoms deteriorating across the emptiness of the vast skies to which we send our prayers, these blasphemies and euphemisms, these imprecations and mumblings that a very old abuse calls "poems." But a star lingers, a polar slant of admiration, of our ardor for the open page turning toward the sky.

Depuis je conjugue, activement je décline – IT
MAY BE WINTER OUTSIDE (BUT IN MY HEART IT'S
SPRING) aussi pauciflorement que possible – les
refrains sont autant de téguments
Enveloppes enveloppes légères je m'enveloppe
when
the temperature dips
langs langsam
trois degrés plus bas
le texte est neigeux fait-il froid
peut-être congèle-t-il à vue d'œil

*À vue d'œil, c'est-à-dire visiblement devant moi dans le temps de
ma lecture, le texte se glace. La page cristallise, sidérée. Elle devient dure
et brillante, translucide, laissant voir à travers son enveloppement de glaçon,
de manière parcimonieuse en même temps que limpide, le spring au cœur du
winter outside. Un très mince et gracile spring, sans efflorescences excessives.
Poème jaloux, réservé, entourant son propre secret pour n'en presque rien
lâcher.*

Because I conjugate, I actively decline – IT
MAY BE WINTER OUTSIDE (BUT IN MY HEART
IT'S SPRING) as paucifloral as possible – the
refrains are all integuments
Envelopes light envelopes I envelop myself in
when
the temperature dips
langs langsam
three degrees lower
the page is snowy it is cold
perhaps it's freezing before our eyes

     At a glance, that is, before my very eyes while I have been reading, the text is freezing. The page crystallizes, dumbstruck. It glitters, hard and translucent, letting us see through its envelope of ice, in a style spare and at the same time limpid, the spring in the heart of the winter outside. A very thin and slender spring, without excessive efflorescence. A reserved, jealous poem, encircling its own secret so almost nothing slips out.

N'importe je re-
sample du Barry White
frain dans le texte c'est la chute.

    Elle sample la voix d'un charmeur black, en sorte qu'à mon tour je peux venir ici sampler parmi ses mots. La poésie sans doute n'est pas à lire, ni à étudier, ni à commenter : mais à sampler. Prélever, couper, remonter, coller, mixer, remixer. Le poème finit l'infini et chaque brique le contient. Lire n'est pas affaire de suivi, c'est une prise instantanée dans un morceau d'image, dans un cristal, dans un glaçon, sur le flanc d'une échappée de pensée. Le poème est écrit en éclats et tel doit être lu. Ou bien tu. Ou su par cœur, en pièces mises bout à bout. À la chance des échantillons. On prend ce qui reste, la chute du refrain. La dernière syllabe, la dernière unité avant la poussière sonore.

    Comme si le poème n'avait d'autre souhait que d'entr'ouvrir une unique syllabe pour y discerner en perspective toutes les galeries des grands signaux verbaux, des belles représentations de sens et de vérité prises en enfilade jusqu'au mur du fond. Un effilement de la voix, une ligne de fuite de lambeaux sonores qui ne cessent de déborder.

Whatever I re-
sample of the Barry White
frain is where the text falls.

She is sampling the voice of a black crooner, so I in turn can come here to sample among her words. Poetry is probably not for reading, studying, or explaining: but for sampling. To pick apart, to cut, to reassemble, to paste, to mix, to remix. The poem completes the infinite and each brick contains it. To read is not a matter of follow-through, it is a snapshot in a part of the image, in a crystal, in an icicle, on the flank of a runaway thought. The poem is written in splinters and one must read it as such. Or be silent. Or have learned by heart, like pieces placed end to end. Chance samplings. One takes what is left, the end of the refrain. The last syllable, the last measure before the resonant dust.

As if the poem had no other wish than to crack open a unique syllable in order to cast into perspective all the galleries of the grand verbal signals, of the beautiful portraits of meaning and truth, one placed after another right up to the wall at the back. A thinning of the voice, a vanishing line of resonant fragments that never cease overflowing.

Longer le mur, compter les briques. Se demander
combien de temps ça prendra. Se dire que ça
prendra le temps que ça prendra.

*Pas plus d'un instant. Le temps de prendre congé. Le temps de
quitter le poème, qui lui-même m'abandonne. On ne continue pas, ça ne
suit pas son cours. Il n'y avait pas de cours. Vous l'avez remarqué. Ça n'a
fait que déborder, sans couler vers aucun estuaire. La philosophie toujours
aboutit à l'océan, lève l'encre et se perd à l'horizon. Le poème rapproche
l'horizon jusqu'à l'embouchure du fleuve, là où il ouvre et ferme sa propre
bouche. On ne quitte pas la terre planétaire. On avale l'eau, toutes les eaux
de Fortino.*

Slide along the wall, count the bricks. Ask
yourself how much time it will take. Tell
yourself that it will take the time it takes.

*No more than an instant. The time it takes to leave. The time it
takes to leave the poem, which itself is deserting me. One doesn't continue,
doesn't follow the course. There was no course to take. You noticed it. All that
it did was to overflow, without flowing into some estuary. Philosophy always
reaches the ocean, weighs ink and is lost on the horizon. The poem brings
the horizon close to the mouth of the river, and there opens and closes its own
mouth. One does not leave the planetary earth. One swallows the water, all
the waters of Fortino.*

La lune, c'est du planétaire, tu l'as bien noté.
Les talus, on leur enlève les barbes à l'aide d'une
faucille, ça s'appelle *barbeyer* ou *disac'her*, j'ai
bien noté que je disac'he depuis des semaines je
barbeye

Herbes après haies fossés feuille forme tige

Pourtant

les mots ne sont pas des étiquettes d'espèce (elles
doivent être en papier blanc ordinaire, collé et un
peu résistant sans être épais) puisque les mots ne
sont pas suffisants (ils ne permettent pas de placer
tous les renseignements nécessaires). Par exemple,
un mot de 0,38 m de long sur 4 à 5 de hauteur ne
suffit pas pour les contenir. Autant que possible,
les mots ne sont pas tous semblables, c'est ce qui
les différencie des étiquettes (les étiquettes ont
intérêt, elles, à être identiques pour les besoins de
l'échantillonnage).

*Les mots sont démesurés, par excès ou par défaut. Le poème leur
donne une commune mesure, que la lecture recalcule à chaque fois. Il faut
maintenant lire à haute voix : For-ti-no Sá-ma-no...*

The moon, you have noticed its planetariness.
The embankments, someone trimmed their beards
with a scythe, call it *to pare down* or *skive
off*, I've noticed I skive off that for weeks I
pare down

Grass then hedge ditch leaf form stem

Yet

words are not a kind of label (those
should be on plain white paper, glued and
a bit sturdy without being too thick) since
words are not enough (they don't allow us
to put in all the necessary pieces of information).
For example, a word 0.38 yards long and 4 to 5
yards high is not large enough to contain them.
As much as possible, words are not all alike,
this is how they differ from labels (it's in the
nature of labels to be identical to meet the needs
of sampling).

    *Words are unmeasurable, in excess or by default. The poem gives
them a common measure, which reading recalculates each time. Now the
poem must be read aloud: For-ti-no Sá-ma-no . . .*

As translators, we have approached this collaborative work especially in relation to crucial aspects of transmission and transpositional exchange fundamental to the original oeuvre. The translation of "the poem, its duplication, and its overflowing" entailed the creation of a poem, its duplication, and its overflowing, we might say, in a parallel universe in English. It has been a heady ride: the process of translation cerebral, its writing physical, practical, in the sense of the *praxis* of translation.

A few specifics are in order about the inevitable, knotty issues that arise in the act of translating. Cole Swensen mentions, in her introduction to the special dossier section of an *Aufgabe* feature on contemporary French poetry (2011), that so much "pressure on the line" has been exerted "that for many [French] writers it has disappeared altogether as a formal principle[.]" Consider Virginie Lalucq's serial poem: There is lineation, with radical line breaks, which at times annotate the text. How do we read and understand these line breaks in order to convey them in English? Some seem meaningful and others don't. How to translate the use of the line? Is lineation even a factor to try to duplicate in translating a poem that does not rhyme, or does not make lineation, as Swensen remarks, a compelling formal principle in the series? The poems are justified in their presentation. Is the justification of lineation to be retained? Such were the questions we asked ourselves as we proceeded.

For the purposes of translation, we noted the typographic element, line breaks which included a number of mid-word breaks, and finally, we decided that following the exploratory nature of both contemporary French and American avant-garde poetries, we would embrace the challenge and explore the meaningful possibilities. That is, we considered this aspect as we worked on the translations, although in practice, we closely tracked—almost like a periplum—the line breaks and justified margins of Lalucq's poems.

Thus, the line endings became a question of interpretative retention for us. As illustration, the following is a characteristic example of what we have termed a *radical* line break in the original:

[. . .] / j'aurai / la bouche / défai-

te / paralysée / gelée [. . .]

The mid-word break has been retained in our translation, because such formal, typo/graphic breakage happens to extend the content in this instance:

[. . .] / my mouth / will freeze / un-

done / paralyzed / [. . .]

We translated such annotative breaks, because form seemed to work hand in hand with meaning. Other broken words, however, seemed not so much to extend the content as to coincide with the justified right margins. In those cases, we decided that to retain the radical line breaks was more misleading than accurate. We therefore quietly lengthened some lines.

We have changed punctuation only in the rare instance, and only for clarity. In addition, we have retained the few instances of lines in other languages (including English), although the admittedly inaccessible Breton (at least for most) we translated into an older English dialect. We (trans)pose this translation as an overflowing of the overflowing of the poem across linguistic boundaries.

A strong thematic element of *Fortino Sámano* (*Les débordements du poème*) is the conversation the two works conduct about the photographic-poetic image, which, though functioning visually, is paradoxically housed only in poetic language. Thus, Nancy's lament that, while the poem is generated out of Lalucq's contemplation of a photograph, the image "says nothing" in the poem, because it is (not) there. Poem and commentary say much about poetry, however, and the contemplation of poetic language so central to this collaborative work is so compelling that we translators never tired of dwelling on it as we labored on the translation for the better part of four years.

The word *language* in English, which is the word we opted to use for most of the occurrences of the word *langue* in French, cannot convey all of the connotations of the French original, which without contorting the poetic moment signifies both *tongue* and *language*. Right there, even on the first page with the epigraph: *mange la langue à l'envers de son acquisition*. This is Jakobson's definition (via Jacques Roubaud) of aphasia, which Rosmarie Waldrop translates as "aphasia devours language in reverse order to its acquisition." Translate *la langue* as *the tongue*, and one has the beginning of a definition of epilepsy, not aphasia. In short, despite the almost bitter loss of the sensuality of the dual meanings, we have followed Waldrop's example, and translated *la langue* (with a very few necessary exceptions based on context) as *language*.

Along those lines, the differences in pronoun usage—most obviously the contrast between the intimacy and formality of the two second person singulars, *tu* and *vous*—simply cannot be translated into English. We contemplated, but finally opted against, excavating *thou*, and made do with translating such moments literally (*you/you*), but here and there we would add a word (*close*, for example) to suggest the intimacy of *tu*. As we noted in the Foreword, Lalucq expressed a strong preference that the literal, essential *meaning* of words be conveyed, and in respecting her wishes, we have tried to balance poetic and substantive considerations as we finalized our translation of her section.

For Nancy's prose explications, where the allusive, associative riffs and wordplays perform as well as house complex poetic analysis—and where to convey the meaning it seems so essential to convey something of the mind's thoughtful, responsive tracking of the poem—we have found parallels which nevertheless closely detail the ripple of lyric invention. To illustrate, we quote from an early passage in Nancy's section, which describes not the absent photographic image, but Lalucq's language, which replaces it:

> *L'image absente, c'est le poème qui fait image en parlant : ainsi « léger liséré de sang » se voit en se lisant, en se disant, se voit littéralement allitéré dans*

*un filet rouge soigneusement brodé. Virginie choisit l'orthographe avec
deux accents aigus plutôt que « liseré » pour insister sur la minceur figée
du filet carmin qui s'ensuivra.*

Because English does not mark its accents, it was out of the question for
us to translate *"accents aigus"* in any meaningful way for English readers.
Our parallel play does *not* in this instance translate the literal meaning,
but it does nevertheless convey the verbal attention Nancy gives to the
text:

> *Absent the image, the poem will make an image in speaking: just as "light
> brim of blood" is seen when read, when said to oneself, seen literally alliterated
> in the carefully elaborated welling of red. Virginie chooses wording that
> doubles blood's plosive, insisting on the coagulating, carmine trickle to follow.*

That is, instead of *two accents*, we cast on *two alliterating plosives*. It isn't
the same, of course, but in arriving at this version, we have duplicated
Nancy's technical, textual attentiveness, the process as well as the
product. Likewise, there is a section of Nancy's commentary which
alludes to a French proverb, *"En avril ne te découvre pas d'un fil,"* which
has a quaint English parallel, "Ne'er cast a clout till May be out." Nancy's
commentary refers to the French proverb, thus to April, but we have
quietly shifted the month to May, to reflect the equivalent proverb in
English. In addition, we felt that an intertextual moment in the Nancy
section—in which he refers to *"Goethe au moment de son exécution,* 'mehr
Licht,'" an occulted allusion less to Goethe's death than to the German
novel, *Goethes Hinrichtung,* by Viktor Glass—was too occluded to be
anything but misleading in English. Therefore, we quietly translated
"exécution" as "death." As it happens, the words *"mehr Licht"* were
reputedly Goethe's last on his deathbed.

Wherever possible, we strove for an exact translation, because
working with living authors demands that the translators subsume
whatever their individual creative bents in the service of conveying as
much of the art of the original as possible. Some would argue that that

transference is not possible at all, but that is a different question than that of a translation's fidelity to the original. When the chasm between the two languages widened and crossing it was in question, we sought the sufficient equivalence—what Ezra Pound termed "the other sort" of (active, interpretive) translation in the service of art. Compelled by the project, we identify with Swensen's characterization of the work of American translators of contemporary French poetry, "keeping [a] bi-cultural friendship alive, but also making it an operative element in American poetry[.]" If translating *Fortino Sámano* (*Les débordements du poème*) has been our aspiration over the years, it has also been our *inspiration*. The words of Virginie Lalucq and Jean-Luc Nancy have changed ours for good.

Virginie Lalucq is part of an emergent generation of experimental feminist poets in France who often work collaboratively, and who draw their material from a wide range of sources and languages. Her poetry has been included in the anthology *Autres territoires*, edited by Henri Deluy (Ferrago/Leo Scheer, 2003), and published in numerous journals. In addition to *Fortino Sámano* (Galilée 2004), she is the author of *Couper les tiges* (Act Mem/Comp'act, 2001). She is a librarian at the National Foundation of the Political Sciences, and lives with her husband and son in Paris.

Jean-Luc Nancy trained in philosophy and science at the Sorbonne and the Institute of Philosophy in Strasbourg. Until 2004, he served as Distinguished Professor of Philosophy at the Université Marc Bloch (Strasbourg). In 2002, Nancy was awarded the "Liberty" Prize by the International Center for Peace in Sarajevo, and in 2005, he was made a Knight of the Legion of Honor in France. He is the author of many books, among the most recent of which, *Au fond des images* (Galilée 2003), was translated into English as *The Ground of the Image* (Fordham UP, 2005).

Sylvain Gallais is a native French speaker transplanted to the U.S. nine years ago. He is currently a professor of Economics and French at Arizona State University. His most recent book is *France Encounters Globalization* (2003). His translation into French of Alberto Rios' novella, *The Curtain of Trees*, was published in Studio (2011), and his co-translations from the French of Virginie Lalucq, Nicole Brossard, and Nathalie Quintaine have appeared in the past two years in *Aufgabe, Interim, American Letters and Commentary*, and *Poetry International*, among others.

Cynthia Hogue has published seven collections of poetry, most recently *Or Consequence* and *When the Water Came: Evacuees of Hurricane Katrina*, both in 2010. She has received Fulbright, NEA (poetry), and NEH (Summer Seminar) Fellowships. In 2005, she was awarded the H.D. Fellowship at the Beinecke Library at Yale University, and in 2008, a MacDowell Colony Residency Fellowship and an Arizona Commission on the Arts Artists Project Grant. In 2010, she received (with Gallais) the Witter Bynner Translation Residency Fellowship from the Santa Fe Art Institute. Hogue holds the Maxine and Jonathan Marshall Chair in Modern and Contemporary Poetry at Arizona State University.

Fortino Sámano (The Overflowing of the Poem)
by Virginie Lalucq and Jean-Luc Nancy
Translated by Sylvain Gallais and Cynthia Hogue

Cover text set in Castellar MT Std.
Interior text set in Garamond Premier Pro.

Cover Art: LIVE TRANSMISSION: movement of the hands of pianist
Martha Argerich while performing Beethoven's Piano Concerto No. 1. 2002.
Graphite on Bristol paper. 28 x 40 inches. www.MorganOHara.com.
© Copyright Morgan O'Hara.

Cover and interior design by Cassandra Smith

Omnidawn Publishing
Richmond, California
2012

Ken Keegan & Rusty Morrison, Co-Publishers & Senior Editors
Cassandra Smith, Poetry Editor & Book Designer
Gillian Hamel, Poetry Editor & OmniVerse Managing Editor
Sara Mumolo, Poetry Editor & OmniVerse New-Work Editor
Peter Burghardt, Poetry Editor & Bookstore Outreach Manager
Turner Canty, Poetry Editor & Features Writer
Jared Alford, Facebook Editor
Juliana Paslay, Bookstore Outreach & Features Writer
Craig Santos Perez, Media Consultant